profitable final

for the

GENERAL PRACTITIONER

Steve Williams AFA FIAB

MAGISTER CONSULTING LTD

Published in the UK by
Magister Consulting Ltd
The Old Rectory
St. Mary's Road
Stone
Dartford
Kent DA9 9AS

Copyright © 2003 Magister Consulting Ltd
Printed in Italy by Fotolito Longo Group

ISBN 1 873839 45 6

About the Author

Steve Williams (AFA, FIAB) is a qualified accountant who has worked within the NHS for over 20 years. He has previously written books on Fundholding and on Making Best Practice Better. He currently provides practice management expertise to many medical practices and also acts as an accountant for GPs. He has worked with PMS Contracts and, more recently, has been assisting doctors to assess the implications of the new GMS Contract.

Steve Williams has also been an associate tutor for the Institute of Health Policy Studies at the University of Southampton and has written many training modules on GP practice.

Acknowledgements

Thank-you to my staff who have supported me with my work within Primary Care for many years, and to all my many clients who I have worked with throughout many periods of dynamic change.

PREFACE

The NHS (and particularly General Practice) continue to transcend the major episodes of reform brought about by the Government White Paper of 1989. More recently the White Papers of 1997 (*Primary Care: Delivering the Future and The New NHS: A Modern and Dependable National Framework*) launched the Primary Care arena into another significant period of transition. These changes have affected the very core of the structure of the NHS, but no single part has been affected more than that of the role of the GP. At a time when most practitioners and their staff were attempting to understand and come to terms with the changes brought about by the GP Contract, a further voluntary reform, the GP Fundholding Scheme, was introduced by the Government. This inclusion in the financial management of general practice made some GPs willingly grasp the opportunity to be more directly involved, both in managing public expenditure and also getting more involved in the true profitability of their own practice.

Others were more reluctant and remained opposed, but still had an obligation, if only to themselves, to take an active interest in the financial running of their practice. The change of government in May 1997 was intended to herald the dawn of a new dependable NHS (that would promote Primary Care Groups) and signalled yet another period of dynamic change. Whilst fundholding was not seen as the preferred option of delivering a primary care led NHS, no single approach was adopted and as a result numerous models were allowed to develop. The introduction of Primary Care Trusts (PCTs) means, in practice, that there is now a real opportunity to contrive to influence the shape and form of the future primary care setting.

The most recent changes have come at a time when, in many cases, there has been a drop in the level of GP remuneration or, in the best cases, only a very slight increase. This trend has been coupled with a general GP recruitment crisis caused by the introduction of new methods of reimbursement together with new rules and regulations laid down in the Statement of Fees and Allowances.

In addition, there have also been new developments that require the GP to take a more proactive approach to the financial running of his or her Practice. For example, electronic data exchange can now link the General Practice with the local PCT, which, in theory, offers the potential to expedite payments. However, in reality, the Practice will need to ensure it has established all the necessary internal controls to check that claims are not being missed and to make sure that all claims are being paid both correctly and promptly.

The potential offered by locally negotiated contracts as part of the Personal Medical Services (PMS) initiative or Primary Care Act Pilots (PCAPs) as they are also known, means that new freedoms and incentives must be managed efficiently if the Practice is to achieve its desired level of profitability. The introduction of the new General Medical Services (GMS) Contract and private sector funding initiatives such as the Local Improvement Finance Trust (LIFT) mean that there is now a significant opportunity for GPs to maximise profit from their personal activities.

General Practice is unique in the world of medicine in that, despite the nature of the work undertaken by the General Practitioner with regard to the GP Contract, it is, in the eyes of the Inspector of Taxes, a business which must be assessed on profits earned and must be taxed accordingly. To this end it is important that the General Practitioner not only knows what income and reimbursements can be claimed, but also which allowances and tax planning measures can be taken to maximise and improve any retained profit. This book provides the answers to those questions. It also elaborates on how best to invest and utilise disposable income while illustrating the successful techniques employed by many people to secure their best long-term interests.

Unlike many other books and summaries on tax and accountancy which tend to generalise, this book looks at only the areas of day-to-day interest to the General Practice, and offers practical advice and techniques for dealing with the operational finances of the busy Practice.

This book acts as a reference guide for those who wish to be involved in the financial management of the Practice. It demonstrates that by good, sound financial control, it is possible to increase the level of retained profit within the Practice and thereby allow future financial planning to be made on a secure footing.

Steve Williams AFA, FIAB

April 2003

CONTENTS

INTRODUCTION

Profit from General Practice activities will be derived directly from efficiency in making claims for income, by correctly claiming reimbursements, by contract negotiation, by tight internal financial control and periodic (but regular) expenditure review.

Ignoring any of these areas will result in potential income loss. Given the amount of administration required and the general bureaucracy involved within General Practice today, it is vitally important that doctors, their managers and professional advisors ensure that they are always fully informed about all changes that affect the Practice. The GP Contract (be it PMS or GMS) and the other NHS reforms have meant that it has been generally recognised that there is now a growing requirement to perceive General Practice as a thriving business, which should be treated as a going commercial concern. This principle is demonstrated by the many practices that have continued to grow and/or merge with smaller practices. Indeed the future of Primary Care may see the demise of the single-hold practitioner. Reforms such as fundholding and the GP commissioning groups were developed to allow consortia arrangements to work. Primary Care Trusts have built on these ideas by bringing GPs together and allowing them to work in collaboration with regard to service provision. Such moves are likely to allow the creation of larger practice groups and this, in turn, would seem to support the adoption of a more business-like approach to General Practice.

In some ways, General Practice operates like other types of trading or service business. As with all businesses, General Practice relies on income and has to control expenditure, however there are two fundamental differences between General Practice and most trading companies:

- Firstly, GPs receive a large proportion of their own income by regular, almost guaranteed payments (and they are members of an occupational pension scheme).

- Secondly, the Practice will be fully reimbursed for certain items of expenditure.

With the introduction of the new General Medical Services (GMS) Contract and the existing Personal Medical Services (PMS) Contracts, more income is being received by the Practice through negotiated local contracts. Although General Practitioners work to the same contracts, invariably no two practices are exactly alike and what works well in one practice may not be suitable or appropriate in another.

The reviewing the financial health of the Practice has tended only to be of real interest to the partners when a new partner is joining or an existing member is retiring. Generally at those times the accounts (with all their complexities) are given a spring clean and very often this can lead to unexpected consequences. To avoid nasty shocks from unforeseen financial problems and to improve future planning, it is vitally important that all partners in the Practice are kept fully informed about the financial status of the Practice. This will help them to contribute to the long-term stability of the Practice as well as influencing their own personal remuneration.

The main aims of this book are:

- To give a clear, jargon-free description of the complexities of the business and financial aspects of General Practice

- To provide clear explanations of the most relevant rules and regulations affecting the Practice and the partners on a regular basis.

To this end, the book will cover all the financial aspects of running a General Practice to help practices obtain maximum profit and then use that profit wisely to secure the most advantageous outcomes. Topics that we will explore include: understanding and applying legislation, cashflow, reducing accountancy fees, maximising income against time actually worked, simple cost efficiency measures and tax planning for partnerships.

Profit is not simply about increasing income or decreasing expenditure. By effectively planning for potential outcomes, unnecessary costs can be avoided and full potential profitability achieved.

CHAPTER 1

INCOME AND EXPENDITURE IN A GP PRACTICE

In this introductory chapter, we set the scene for our discussion of financial management in a GP practice. We explore the current and forthcoming legislation that governs General Practice and the types of income and expenditure that are experienced in all practices.

GMS versus PMS

At the time of writing this book, everyone is anticipating the introduction of the new General Medical Services Contract. The Personal Medical Services Contracts have been in existence now for a few years now and there is still a lot of deliberation amongst medical practitioners about the benefits of such arrangements. Whichever way Primary Care goes, it is clear that this moment in time offers a definite window of opportunity to assess one's practice income sources and determine the most profitable solution for the future.

The new Contracts are being offered to assist in controlling central costs by converting previously unlimited cash resources into cash-limited resources. What this offers the medical practitioner is an opportunity to agree to a contract that benefits him or her both financially and hours worked.

However, if the Contract is not suitable at the outset, it will be increasingly difficult to access new monies. For example, there are cases where practices are still waiting to be reimbursed for claims. In one case, a practice made a claim two years ago and to date no adjustment has been made to its contract baseline. The Practice applied for additional funding due to additional services being provided and a significant increase in list size.

Difficulty accessing new monies has already been experienced under the early PMS Contracts, where discussions still take place about contract variations and exceptional circumstances. In many cases, genuine claims for monies do not necessarily mean additional funds. In the case illustrated, the practice provided services to a larger population for no extra funding and its additional services are being funded directly by the practice principal themselves.

It is important for the GP to understand the main components of any Primary Care Contract and the best place to start with that process is to look at the system that is about to be replaced, namely the Statement of Fees and Allowances (SFAs). The existing Contract, governed by the SFAs, will be replaced by the new GMS Contract that will effectively subsume the SFAs. PMS Contracts will run alongside the new GMS Contract. PMS Contracts already allow freedom from the constraints of the SFAs.

Income Sources and Remuneration Levels

Anyone who wants to maximise profit within General Practice must take the time to understand and evaluate the contents of the Statement of Fees and Allowances (otherwise known more commonly the 'Red Book'). Even with the introduction of local PMS and GMS Contracts, understanding the basis of any funding will be critical to ensuring that income potential is not lost. The reasoning behind this is simple. Contained within these pages are the general rules and principles covering the recovery of costs and the payment of fees to GPs. However, this issue is also critical because with the new PMS Contracts and the forthcoming GMS Contract, effectively all these regulations and legislation form part of the terms of service of the General Practitioner. To that end it is important that at least one person in the Practice, but preferably two, are made responsible for updating this information and thereby ensuring that the rules and regulations are reviewed and kept current. One obvious benefit of doing this is that this will help to ensure that all potential and legitimate claims can be made. In past years, this kind of information was not widely available outside the Practice, which often led to confusion when accounts were being prepared. Today, there are firms of accountants who have specialist knowledge of General Practice and there are those who keep fully up to date with the changes affecting the SFAs and local Contracts.

Understanding the key areas of income is critical to managing a successful practice. Ignorance can not be used as an excuse for not achieving all possible profit potential within the Practice. It should be remembered that more and more of GP income is based on capitation criteria. Therefore, it is no longer prudent to have a number of patients under question with the local Trust. In some cases where patients live in boundary areas, they are often not registered with the relevant trust. This means that a practice may see patients and apply for them to be on their list, but the authority can not locate them as they are deemed as being in another authority area. Very often these people are referred to as 'ghost patients'.

Unresolved issues relating to the registration of patients will be costing the Practice money. In the past, under the control of Family Practitioner Committees, much of the calculation and, indeed the claiming of allowances, was carried out on behalf of the General Practice. With the creation of Family Health Services Authorities (FHSAs), a change of working practices meant that more allowances were paid on information available with more use of random review of payments. Practices would provide certain data and payments were made on this basis. The Authority would randomly check claims rather than calculating every single claim.

The abolition of FHSAs and the enabling legislation giving the new style Primary Care Trusts overall management responsibilities has led to further changes. Therefore, there was a greater reliance on the

Practice to make sure that all possible claims were being made. Latterly, with the age of the computer and electronic links, we are seeing the move to the computerised management of the flow of claims and payments between the Practice and the Trust. However, even the most sophisticated systems need to be reviewed and in particular where it applies to potential income to the Practice, it is the responsibility of the Practice to ensure that it has the internal and financial controls to manage the situation. Whether the Practice elects to add a PMS Contract or chooses a local, new GMS Contract, it will be vital that the Practice understands the basic components of what makes up income. Previous non-cash-limited sums will be transferred into cash-limited votes of money and therefore, if the Contract is not set at the optimum value at the outset, it could be difficult to increase any sum in the future.

The Basic Practice Allowance

This is the first type of allowance we will describe and, surprisingly enough, it relates to the number of patients in the Practice. GPs achieving the appropriate number of patients will qualify for this allowance. The way this allowance is derived is that a higher allowance is given for the first 400 patients and then as numbers increase the allowance decreases to the maximum allowed. This principle means that the allowance is weighted in favour of the smaller patient list and reflects the proportionally weighted expenses associated with such a practice. GPs working part-time also attract a weighted element to this allowance. Thus it has already become clear that a GP with many patients can actually be eligible for less allowances than a GP with fewer patients due to the weighting factor.

Payments for Deprivation

The ways in which the system defines, measures and makes payments for deprivation have always been an area of contention. No matter where it is used, the Jarman Index (a standard method for measuring deprivation and for calculating the allowances for individual practices) appeared to have certain inconsistencies and many practices felt that it did not provide an accurate reflection of their own Practice demographics. Certainly in inner city areas, there can often be many small pockets of deprivation intermingled with affluent areas. Even though the Practice may have been given a certain score according to the Jarman Index, there may be scope within the Practice to negotiate with the local authority to obtain additional funding in proven cases of genuine deprivation not recognised under the current ranking. Very often Primary Care Trusts (PCTs) will adopt their own local deprivation indicators to assist in allocating appropriate funding. However, such funding very often does not account for demographic change over a number of years.

Payments for Seniority

How often does your Practice review seniority payments? In theory, it does not seem a major issue, but if you forget when a partner is due to switch between bands, it is possible that those income opportunities may be missed. The key factors about seniority payments is how long the individual has been registered as a GP and how long they have been providing GMS services. Part-time GPs still attract a *pro-rata* payment and there are special rules for job-sharers.

Capitation-Based Fees

This element is quite critical as it combines both the number of patients but also gives different types of patients a weighting factor. For example, in particular it distinguishes between patients of different ages (those patients to age 65, those over 65 and aged to 74 and finally those aged 75 and over). Interestingly enough, whilst those patients aged 75 and over attract a higher fee, it is meant to reflect the increased level of services being provided to this age group. However, even though this age group attracts a higher allowance, they may not necessarily be the highest income group for the Practice. A popular type of patient for a practice is the young couple intending to settle down and start a family. These types of patient are likely to require relatively uncomplicated services from the Practice for at least the next five to six years after starting their family.

Patient Registration Fee

This was introduced to ensure that all new patients joining a practice list received particular attention. Whilst not completely successful, it has helped many practices to focus upon their existing list of patients and set up protocols for accepting patients onto their list. The practice should attempt to analyse their practice profile and therefore attempt to ascertain the most appropriate patients for their particular list.

Education Payments

GPs are very fortunate that they can claim for expenses relating to post-graduate education courses. GPs may claim reimbursement for such courses by means of the Post-graduate Education Allowance (PGEA). There is an obvious need for continuing professional education and this allowance is designed to meet course, travel and subsistence costs. Broadly the education allowance falls into three categories:

- Health promotion and illness prevention

- Disease management

- Service management

To qualify for the allowance the practitioner must provide evidence that at least an average of five days per year have been achieved over a five-year period. Therefore if a claim is submitted and at least 25 days training has been completed with at least two days per each category, then the payments will be made quarterly into the next financial period. Special rules also apply for single-handed practitioners who wish to use locum cover to attend training. This is a payment type that seems uncomplicated, but there have been incidences where training allowance claims have been submitted that did not meet the criteria (eg: the course was listed as 'PGEA approval sought', but none was ever given) or the practice had not kept a proper register of course dates and therefore missed out on qualifying for payments because of timing differences.

Childhood Immunisation and Cervical Cytology

This is an interesting area. Introduced to give an incentive for practices to work towards certain targets, allowances for childhood immunisation and cervical cytology appear to be a sensible way of encouraging practices to achieve and be rewarded for their achievement. When the rules were first introduced, they were clearly meant to act as an incentive for practices to achieve the higher targets. For childhood immunisations, the allowances were 70% for lower targets and 90% for higher targets. For cervical cytology the allowances were 50% and 80% respectively. Interestingly, once the higher target of say 90% is achieved, no further payments are paid. Therefore a practice achieving 100% is no better off than one achieving 90%. It follows that a practice should monitor its patient list to achieve the higher targets, but not to unnecessarily over-achieve such targets during any one claim period.

Child Health Surveillance Fees

To qualify for payments for child health surveillance, first the Practitioner must apply to be included on the child health surveillance list. The GP must be able to demonstrate the appropriate ability and experience. A supplement payment is then made to the GP for each child under the age of five who is receiving developmental surveillance from the GP.

Minor Surgery Payments

Again, as above, the GP needs to be included in the minor surgery list and this allows the opportunity for those appropriately qualified and experienced to carry out certain procedures and receive the appropriate payment. This can be quite a good income source for a larger Partnership, if the Partners agree that the minor surgery is carried out by one Partner and the claim is made for the Partnership. This takes away the need for re-training and provides an opportunity for developing quality in the service provision.

Health Promotion

The recent rules concerning health promotion clinics and the introduction of bandings means that a practice should be looking at ways of achieving or maintaining the top level band. The move towards as Primary Care led NHS and the use of a number of practitioners (such as developing the role of the practice nurse and the running of outreach clinics) has meant that there are more opportunities to develop clinics and protocols to meet the payment criteria.

Teaching Allowance

Where a practice decides to assist universities to train under-graduate medical students by allowing them to carry out work experience within the General Practice, then an allowance is payable subject to the number of students and how long they are actually at the Practice.

Night Visits

This is an area of particular concern, as Practice claims are often queried. Many GPs deal with a number of their night time calls over the telephone, thereby not actually going out to make that many night visits. Different arrangements have been made all over the country: from the use of relief services, to practices working in co-operatives and even incidences of full-time GPs being employed purely to cover night work. The Practice should look at all the local options and ensure that it chooses the most time-saving and cost-effective solution for their own particular needs.

Other Allowances and Managing Claims

The above are the key allowances, but there are many more including:

- Associate allowance
- Employment of an assistant
- Payments for prolonged sickness
- Prolonged study leave
- Rural practice allowance
- Maternity medical services
- Inducement fees
- Trainee practitioner payments.

The above represent but a few of the available allowances and help to demonstrate that, whereas a commercial business might have a very specific range of products to sell, with General Practice the way in which income is computed can be very complicated. Consequently, it is important to remain alert if you want to guarantee that your Practice is claming everything that can be claimed. It is not just important to ensure that the Practice is claiming the correct level of fees, but if it claims incorrectly (and therefore receives too large a figure for allowances), then the Trusts have the power to instigate proceedings to recover this money and effectively prevent the GP concerned from practising. Therefore, the simple rule to follow should be to get it right first time, get paid promptly (and in the earliest available period) and never do work unnecessarily through bad planning of Practice resources.

The sole Practitioner is obviously the most limited in terms of time and resources and, therefore, must plan very carefully the areas of work to be undertaken, so that they will fulfil the terms of the GP contract while, at the same time, maximising income. The Partnership can look to share the load and draw upon particular skills and abilities, but should also be careful that work of the Partners does not overlap while ensuring that the majority of the workload does not fall on one particular GP.

The government change in 1997 indicated, albeit tentatively, that the future of the NHS will be Primary Care driven. Already we have seen an expanded interpretation of the 'Red Book' and there are many local and regional initiatives being introduced which allow GPs, with Primary Care Trust approval, to carry out and be remunerated for an increasing range of services above and beyond their normal core GMS activities. It is imperative for the Practice to be proactive and review its potential options now. Change always leads to financial opportunities. The new GMS Contract is such an opportunity.

To conclude: to understand the complexities of the GMS Contract could take a long time to comprehend and therefore interpret correctly – an additional pressure for GPs who are already very busy and pressurised. One of the easiest ways of looking for profit is to select a particular area of income and check to see whether all appropriate claims are being made and to see whether there is any room for improvement. Regular reviews and audit of Practice claims will identify trends and potential shortcomings in the Practice. Never lose the incentive to review Practice income.

Commentary

Contact both your local Primary Care Trust and Local Health Authority to obtain details about any initiatives in your area to carry out and be remunerated for services beyond the normal core GMS activities. Constantly review press releases from the Department of Health to identify new potential sources of income.

With the introduction of self-assessment, less reliance is placed on Practice accounts for tax computations. The introduction of the self-assessment scheme meant that all taxpayers are dealt with on the same basis, with the aim of bringing all taxpayers' affairs up-to-date. There is no reason why any medical practitioner should not have their tax affairs completely up-to-date. The future of tax assessment and general PAYE (Pay as Your Earn) matters will be dealt with by filing accounts electronically with the Inland Revenue. An accountant is not a statutory requirement to carry out this function and each doctor must realise that he or she is the only one who is ultimately responsible for their own tax affairs and tax liability. Using specialist accountants can sometimes be cost-effective. Not only can they assist in maximising income sources for the Practice, but also they often charge fixed fees because they can anticipate the needs of the Practice as a result of their specific knowledge and experience of financial and tax affairs within General Practice. However, do remember that all the financial management practices covered in this book could be done effectively by the GP Practice itself and if outside accountancy services are employed, the cost incurred should be considered in relation to the overall profitability of the Practice.

CHAPTER 2

FINANCIAL MANAGEMENT ISSUES - PART I

Basic Accounting Principles

Introduction

Whatever the type of business, one aspect is common: that is the language of money. General Practice is ultimately driven by money – and the nature and size of a practice will be reflected in the overall financial stability of the organisation. Even the smallest of practices can usually demonstrate turnover that exceeds a six-figure sum and many large health centres have extremely high levels of turnover.

A commercial business must eventually understand and keep good accounting records. Without these, the business has the potential to fail and is likely to incur significant costs such as high accountancy fees. The nature of the GP Contract (and the process of regular claims and receipts) has meant that an attitude is often seen in practice that reflects an absence of urgency when it comes to financial matters. The PMS and, potentially, the new locally negotiated GMS contract will create a budget-led contract. This means that practices will now know in advance their total annual income. This could lead to complacency and therefore potential lost income. This is not true of all practices, but many practices still rely on inexperienced or unsuitably qualified staff to manage their finances. This chapter aims to concisely cover the key accounting principles in order that more sense can be made of the key financial processes occurring in the Practice.

The New GP

When a GP retires or leaves a practice, very often replacements are found from those wishing to enter General Practice. The expectancy today, even more so than in the past, is to obtain parity in the form of equal partnership status in the shortest possible time. In order for there to be clear understanding between both the existing doctors and the incoming doctor, not only should a Partnership Agreement be drawn up, but a clear understanding of the financial status of the Practice must be known. For example, very often decisions about joining a practice are made on the most recently available accounts, which can often be for a period ending many months previously.

The Existing GP

Again, when there is a change of partnership, it is vitally important for the existing doctors to fully understand the financial status of the Practice or it could be possible for costly errors to occur. Such errors can take a long time to resolve and in turn could lead to unnecessary loss of earnings. The easiest way to resolve such dilemmas is to grasp a basic understanding of accounting principles and consistently apply them.

Decisions based on financial outcomes are made constantly within General Practice and although the Practice may employ an accounts assistant, Practice Manager or bookkeeper, there is still a need for the doctors themselves to understand the financial consequences of their ultimate actions and decisions. Such decisions could include matters concerning:

- Actual cash
- Partners' drawings
- Staff payments
- Employment legislation

- Financial controls

- Budgets

- Taxation

- Insurance

- Banking facilities

- Investments

- Property

The above is but a sample of the types of issues that a practice may deal with on a daily basis and in order to remain in control, the Practice must have access to well-maintained and up-to-date accounting records.

Why Keep Records?

There are a number of obvious reasons for keeping records, but there are also many other uses for and benefits from the keeping of accurate financial records, for example:

- To monitor Practice income and thereby determine areas of potential growth and areas that are not so profitable

- To determine how much GMS work is profitable above the minimum requirement and whether to look at alternative methods of income generation

- To analyse spending patterns and therefore take control of fixed and variable expenditure

- By using a combination of all of the above, determine profit levels with a view to ultimately maximising profit for all the partners

- To fulfil statutory obligations in respect of the Inland Revenue (self-assessment) and to effect Partnership Agreements

- To reduce Practice accountancy fees by maintaining clear records yourself

- To provide up-to-date information to assist with day-to-day decision making

- To give all the doctors peace of mind and the ability to forward plan.

Out of all the examples given above, perhaps the one that offers the most immediate savings to the Practice is the use of good bookkeeping and record keeping to help to reduce accountancy fees. The more records the Practice completes themselves (and the more information they produce) the less routine work will need to be carried out by the Practice accountants and potentially a large slice of the annual fee could be saved. All too often, the accountant is given incomplete records or vouchers that are not filed or reconciled. This basic type of housekeeping work is not a cost-efficient use of your accountant's time, but the Practice will still be billed for it. If the Practice spend time doing the basics, the accounts preparation becomes easier and the accountant can then be used, if required, to look at tax planning and other ways of cost improvement within the Practice.

The Financial Records

Generally, the Practice will keep two types of financial records: one will be petty cash and the other will be the main Practice cash book. The Practice should set a policy about the types of items that will be reimbursed through the petty cash system. Normally it is sensible to set a financial limit to the amount that any one individual can draw on a given day or over a period of perhaps a week. Where petty cash vouchers are not received, a petty cash slip should definitely be signed and indeed it is good practice for all recipients of petty cash to sign a receipt.

The normal method adopted for operating a petty cash system is called the 'Imprest System'. This is where the Practice starts with a given value and as money is withdrawn, it is replenished (say at the end of month) to the original value of the petty cash float.

Example of the 'Imprest System' for operating and recording petty cash:

Opening Float	£100.00
Travel Expense	£12.50
Parking	£3.00
Stationery	£27.80
Closing Balance:	**£56.70**
Amount required to replenish float:	**£43.30**

The appropriate vouchers or signed receipts should be kept safely. Very often the petty cash account is incorrectly used to account for other cash receipts in the Practice. For example, using the petty cash to pay a cleaner or a casual member of staff would certainly be an action that would be scrutinized by the Inland Revenue in the event of an investigation. Whenever possible, all Practice related receipts should be paid into the Practice bank account. Should the Practice be subject to an Inland Revenue inspection or review, it is likely that petty cash will be analysed and the inclusion of such income or payment to staff will warrant detailed examination.

Some practices can carry large petty cash floats and it is therefore important that regular and random reconciliations of the physical cash are made. It has not be unknown for members of staff to 'borrow' funds and whilst it may always be the intention to pay the money back, such an occurrence is fraudulent and displays a breach of trust. The petty cash accounting records can be manual, but with the computerisation of General Practice and the use of accounting software, the latter is becoming more common place. The easiest rule to apply is to set the petty cash float at a sensible and reasonable level and not to allow exceptions to this.

One approach to take would be to look at the items that are purchased using petty cash (and why) and then analyse these costs to see if using petty cash in this way is cost-effective. For example, petty cash is often used to purchase large amounts of postage or stationery and may involve a member of the staff leaving the premises to make these purchases. The time away from the premises is a hidden cost to the employer who is paying for that time in the person's salary. It could be that it would be more cost-effective to avoid using petty cash for such purchases in order to enable that member of staff to remain in the Practice premises and to make more effective use of their time.

When the petty cash book is written up it should be analysed by expenditure types which correspond to those shown in the main cash book. A computerised system will automatically create this link for you.

The Main Cash Book

Like the petty cash book, the main cash book will be written up to analyse both income and expenditure and should provide extra detail such as invoice numbers and cheque numbers. Very often a reference number is entered into the cash book which corresponds with a number written on the actual invoice. This makes for ease of reference. When the cash book has been written up it should represent all income received and expenditure paid according to when it has actually been received or paid. As such the cash book is not truly representative of the actual profit and loss situation of the Practice. This is because no account is taken for debtors or creditors in the cash book. A debtor is where an invoice has been raised by the Practice or a claim issued and remains unpaid at a given time. A creditor is where the Practice has been invoiced and supplied goods or services but has yet to pay for them. If the Practice is using a computerised system it is possible to account for such items as the system will generate a trial balance, profit and loss account and balance sheet. However, in the absence of such software, the Practice should keep a manual system. One of the easiest ways is to keep the 'unpaid' invoices separate in a box file. This can be analysed at any time to produce a summary of the debtor/creditor position. The information in the cash book should again be totalled and reconciled to the bank statement on a monthly basis.

Accounting Software

Many practices have not considered using accounting software but, as previously stated, the General Practice is comparable to a small business and, in most cases, will deal with more transactions than a lot of commercial small businesses. Computerised systems can be updated daily and the process becomes more a case of data entry rather than bookkeeping. Given that most practices (and almost certainly in the future, all practices) will have computers, it seems logical to purchase accounting software. This idea becomes all the more attractive when you consider that the cost is often less than £100.00 and, if purchased outright and used correctly, the software will probably pay for itself during its first year. Remember that it should be possible to reduce accountancy fees if the accounts preparation work is done in the Practice.

The real advantage of a computerised system is that it will produce your cash book, a trial balance, a profit and loss account and a balance sheet. It can, therefore, reduce the time it takes to produce interim or annual accounts. With the introduction of self-assessment (covered later in this book) and in particular the rules governing partnerships, it will become even more important to obtain timely and accurate information.

With the introduction of automatic payments between the new authorities and the General Practice, it would seem logical to evaluate all financial requirements to ensure that you have a computer system that is completely compatible with that used by your Local Health Authority and/or Trust – and one which allows flexibility as far as management and financial control. If a computerised system is used, it should not be forgotten that the data coming out is only as good as the data going in, therefore procedures and controls should be reviewed regularly.

The Trial Balance

The trial balance represents the accumulation of all account types (whether income and expenditure or otherwise). Under the rules of double entry bookkeeping (where for each entry there is a contra entry) the sum of all the debits and credits shown in the trial balance should always be equal or, alternatively, all the debits less all the credits should total zero. If that is not the case, then the double entry has not been protected and this will mean a detailed review may need to be made, which again could cost the Practice in fees. A computerised system will always follow the double entry rule and therefore should make the likelihood of incomplete records almost impossible. A manual system will always be susceptible to error or mis-posting, and the possibility of such errors occurring reinforces the reason why it is so important to regularly reconcile the cash book.

The trial balance can be analysed to identify which items fall into the categories of income and expenditure or profit and loss – and the remaining accounts or items will represent the balance sheet accounts. Each category can be given a code and then, by analysing these categories the accounts can be prepared and results identified. The principal of double entry bookkeeping is protected in the trial balance. If an amount is entered in one place, it requires that a contra entry is entered to maintain the equal balance between the varied accounts.

Conclusion

One of the most important aspects about understanding the principles of accounting is to remember to keep it as simple as possible. Remember that there is no scientific wizardry to accounting. The principles used today are the same as those used hundreds of years ago when the concept of double entry bookkeeping was first introduced. The only complications faced by people today are the complications that they create themselves. Keep it simple! For every entry, there is a contra entry or, to put it another way, for every action, there will be a re-action! If you have a basic understanding of accounting principles, you will be able to deal with accounting codes and 'charts of accounts'. If you are not familiar with these concepts, there are software products on the market today, which remove the need to understand the principles and rely only on good data entry skills. Inevitably, all practices will use computers more and more and it follows that the accounting function will be absorbed into this.

Very often a manual system will not be reconciled, items will be omitted and no account will be taken of items such as business expenditure paid personally by a doctor. This means it becomes difficult to actually produce up-to-date information and often the information produced is misleading. The computerisation of all aspects of practice finance is a sensible way forward, whether done in the Practice or provided externally. It should reduce your accountancy fees and provide you with good management information. The introduction of a computerised system will need to be complimented by sound internal and financial controls. It is a relatively cheap option to implement and could be saving you money within the first year.

CHAPTER 3

FINANCIAL MANAGEMENT ISSUES - PART II

Keeping Cashflow under Control

Introduction

The purpose of this chapter is to look at the concept of cash accounting, the importance of developing good cash management and the use of cashflow forecasts. A practice may be profitable but, without good sound cashflow management controls, it can be in danger of missing out on its potential to achieve maximum profits.

Cashflow revolves around the actual receipt and payment of monies irrespective of when the profit is earned or the loss is incurred. Good cash management will ensure that profits continue to rise, whilst improper control will generate unnecessary losses and slowly, but surely, erode away at overall profits.

Accounts

The production of the Practice accounts is intended to demonstrate the overall performance of the Practice in money terms by illustrating to the owners of the Practice (namely the doctors) how well they and their staff have managed the Practice affairs. More currently with the introduction of the PMS Contract and new local GMS Contract there is a greater need to understand the technical requirements of accounts and therefore formally accept ownership and take responsibility. Under the new Contract, such accounts will be more closely under the scrutiny of the Primary Care Trust who will exercise their own decisions and judgments about the performance of the Practice. It is not unknown for such organisations to exercise their rights for access to the Practice accounts, which in turn places a greater emphasis on the Practice to ensure that their accounting controls and records are completely up-to-date.

In general, accounts will be drawn up on a historical basis, which means that they are compiled using information about what was actually spent and received. This form of accounting does not attempt to value the Practice. Very often the balance sheet position will represent an approximate asset value. Asset value is usually a price that has been calculated using depreciation and will not necessarily reflect the "true price", ie: price you could ask for an item or the Practice if you sold them today. The asset value of the Practice will not reflect the true price unless there has been a recent change to the practice such as the following:

- **The Practice might re-value their assets (such as property) where there has been significant inflationary changes**

- **A partnership change**

- **Change in the personal circumstances of the partners, such as illness**

In the case of property, such re-valuations should be done with a specific purpose in mind and not simply to make the balance sheet look healthier. In recent years, some GPs found themselves caught in a negative equity trap due to the fact that the assets of their practices (particularly property) did not reflect market changes and district valuations. It is important that the correct valuations are taken and agreed whenever there are changes in the Partnership to avoid disputes arising and unnecessary costs being incurred.

Who Manages Cashflow?

The size of the Practice and the numbers of doctors and staff will often determine who plays a key role in managing cashflow. As the smaller Practice grows, the doctors will find that they have less and less free time available to deal with financial matters. Hence, the responsibilities are passed to managers and staff to run various parts of the Practice. Many doctors are only really interested in the professional management and medical aspect of their practice. To this end, it means that there will be in General Practice a clear separation of ownership and financial management. In the larger Practice there may be a lead GP who liaises with the accountant on financial issues. For the smaller partnership and sole practitioners, there often is a miscomprehension about the role of the accountant, often summed up by the expression:

"but isn't that what I pay an accountant for?"

Your accountant will act as your agent, help prepare your accounts and agree your tax liabilities with the Inland Revenue, but the less information you give him, the more your accountant's fee will be. Therefore it follows that the more work that the GP Practice can do in-house, the easier it will be to control the accountant's fees, because there will be no duplication of effort. Very often, a lot of time is spent by practice staff preparing information, only to find that the accountants completely recast the information because it is not in an acceptable format to them. Remember that a sole practitioner or a partnership does not have to employ the services of an accountant, because they can elect to act for themselves. The happy medium really is to do as much financial work as possible in the Practice and then to use your accountant to liaise with the Inland Revenue as well as working with your Practice to look at ways of improving profit and increasing efficiency.

Cashflow and How It Affects Profit

Most transactions will have a true cash effect and will be recorded as such. There are specific exceptions such as depreciation. However, if accounts were prepared to reflect only cash transactions, they could prove to be very misleading. This is particularly true in General Practice, as not all practices have the same standard year end date. General Practice (in common with commercial organisations) revolves around certain transactions being undertaken on the basis of giving and receiving credit. However, there is another aspect to General Practice in as much as certain items are reimbursable. To show the income but not account for the expenditure would cause the profit to be overstated and therefore taxation would be levied unnecessarily. Therefore in order to ensure that the accounts are not misleading it is necessary to adjust the accounts to ensure that the opinion reached is deemed as 'True and Fair'. The following are examples of such items:

Credit services:

When a doctor raises an invoice or places a claim for reimbursement, a debtor arises and the cash payment may be received sooner or later. (There is a wide variation nationally about performance of former FHSAs, now part of the new style Health Agencies). When the cash is actually received will depend on how well the Practice manages its credit control procedures. When it comes to being paid on time, remember that, if you don't ask, you don't get! Just because an amount is due, doesn't always mean that the money will arrive soon.

Prepayments:

This is particularly relevant to General Practice as there are many costs that fall into this category. Insurance premiums are a good example of prepayments. Very often premiums are paid in advance and therefore if an adjustment is not made, then the appropriate part of the cost will not be allocated into the appropriate year.

Accruals:

As with prepayments, there may be costs for which the Practice has yet to pay or receive an invoice. Normally such transactions cover utilities bills such as rates, water rates, electricity and gas. Failure to accrue for the correct proportion of costs could result in profit being overstated and therefore tax liabilities overstated.

The Bank

Good cash management will be respected and appreciated by your bank manager. Bank managers are seen by GPs as another unnecessary evil but, if approached sensibly, a good working relationship can be developed and many problems avoided. Very often it is the late reimbursement of funds that causes the Practice temporary financial hardship. However, one telephone call to the bank manager can often ease the way and prevent the Practice suffering excessive bank charges. In any case, if the Practice suffers avoidable bank charges due to the incorrect reimbursement of monies or the tardiness of payment, then the proactive Practice should look to seek compensation for such costs and therefore not be out of pocket.

What Do The Banks Look For?

Most bank managers, although not all, are aware of the relative security and therefore low risk of General Practice. However, a practice with a continuing need to use and/or increase its overdraft facility will attract the same pressures and scrutiny as an ailing commercial business. Banks will not guarantee overdrafts indefinitely and can recall an overdraft facility on demand.

The bank manager will ask for evidence of two key documents in conjunction with the published accounts of the Practice. These are namely:

- The Operating Budget

- The Cashflow Forecast

The key distinction between the two types of reports is that the budget defines what the predicted profit or loss of the practice will be (normally shown month by month) and the cashflow forecast determines the actual cash requirements of the practice (again shown month by month). These reports are easy to produce and can easily be developed using a spreadsheet. The tables overleaf detail how a typical example might look for a general practice:

Tables

Table 1: THE OPERATING BUDGET

Month / Figures rounded to £s	April Budget	April Actual	May Budget	May Actual	June Budget	June Actual	July Budget	July Actual	August Budget	August Actual	September Budget	September Actual
Income												
1 Cash	£ 5,100.00		£ 5,100.00		£11,050.00		£15,300.00		£17,000.00		£ 6,800.00	
2 Credit												
a Total Sales (1+2)	£ 5,100.00	£ -	£ 5,100.00	£ -	£11,050.00	£ -	£15,300.00	£ -	£17,000.00	£ -	£ 6,800.00	£ -
Variable Costs												
3 Purchase of goods or materials used												
Purchases - Goods	£ 1,530.00		£ 1,530.00		£ 3,315.00		£ 4,590.00		£ 5,100.00		£ 2,040.00	
4 Wages and Salaries	£ 600.00		£ 600.00		£ 1,300.00		£ 1,800.00		£ 2,000.00		£ 800.00	
b Total variable costs (3+4)	£ 2,130.00	£ -	£ 2,130.00	£ -	£ 4,615.00	£ -	£ 6,390.00	£ -	£ 7,100.00	£ -	£ 2,840.00	£ -
c Gross profit [a - b]	£ 2,970.00	£ -	£ 2,970.00	£ -	£ 6,435.00	£ -	£ 8,910.00	£ -	£ 9,900.00	£ -	£ 3,960.00	£ -
d Gross profit as % of sales [c ÷ a x 100]	58%		58%		58%		58%		58%		58%	
Fixed Costs												
5 Overheads production												
6												
11 Selling and distribution												
13												
17 Administration												
19 Sundry Expenses	£ 253.00		£ 253.00		£ 253.00		£ 253.00		£ 253.00		£ 253.00	
23 Other expenses												
Rent/rates	£ 500.00		£ 500.00		£ 500.00		£ 500.00		£ 500.00		£ 500.00	
Heating/Lighting	£ 208.00		£ 208.00		£ 208.00		£ 208.00		£ 208.00		£ 208.00	
Insurance	£ 83.00		£ 83.00		£ 83.00		£ 83.00		£ 83.00		£ 83.00	
Repairs	£ 1,500.00		£ -		£ -		£ -		£ -		£ -	
Cleaning	£ 8.33		£ 8.33		£ 8.33		£ 8.33		£ 8.33		£ 8.33	
Telephone	£ 30.00		£ 30.00		£ 30.00		£ 30.00		£ 30.00		£ 30.00	
Professional Fees	£ 200.00		£ -		£ -		£ -		£ -		£ 200.00	
Depreciation	£ 415.00		£ 415.00		£ 415.00		£ 415.00		£ 415.00		£ 415.00	
25												
29 Finance charges	£ 583.00		£ 583.00		£ 583.00		£ 583.00		£ 583.00		£ 583.00	
e Total fixed costs	£ 3,780.33	£ -	£ 2,080.33	£ -	£ 2,080.33	£ -	£ 2,080.33	£ -	£ 2,080.33	£ -	£ 2,280.33	£ -
f Net profit before tax [c - e]	(£ 810.33)	£ -	£ 889.67	£ -	£ 4,354.67	£ -	£ 6,829.67	£ -	£ 7,819.67	£ -	£ 1,679.67	£ -
g Sales you need to break even [e ÷ d x 100]	£ 6,491.48		£ 3,572.39		£ 3,572.39		£ 3,572.39		£ 3,572.39		£ 3,932.23	

Month Figures rounded to £s	October Budget	October Actual	November Budget	November Actual	December Budget	December Actual	January Budget	January Actual	February Budget	February Actual	March Budget	March Actual	Total Budget	Total Actual
Income														
1 Cash	£ 5,100.00		£ 5,100.00		£ 3,400.00		£ 3,400.00		£ 3,400.00		£ 4,250.00		£85,000.00	£ -
2 Credit													£ -	£ -
a Total Sales...	£ 5,100.00		£ 5,100.00		£ 3,400.00		£ 3,400.00		£ 3,400.00		£ 4,250.00		£85,000.00	£ -
Variable...														
3 Purchase of...													£ -	£ -
Purchases...	£ 1,530.00		£ 1,530.00		£ 1,020.00		£ 1,020.00		£ 1,020.00		£ 1,275.00		£25,500.00	£ -
4 Wages...	£ 600.00		£ 600.00		£ 400.00		£ 400.00		£ 400.00		£ 500.00		£10,000.00	£ -
b Total var...	£ 2,130.00	£ -	£ 2,130.00	£ -	£ 1,420.00	£ -	£ 1,420.00	£ -	£ 1,420.00	£ -	£ 1,775.00	£ -	£35,500.00	£ -
c Gross prof...	£ 2,970.00	£ -	£ 2,970.00	£ -	£ 1,980.00	£ -	£ 1,980.00	£ -	£ 1,980.00	£ -	£ 2,475.00	£ -	£49,500.00	£ -
d ...as % of...	58%		58%		58%		58%		58%		58%		58%	
Fixed Costs														
5 Overheads...													£ -	£ -
6														
11 Selling...													£ -	£ -
13														
17 Admin...														
19 Sundry Exp...	£ 253.00		£ 253.00		£ 253.00		£ 253.00		£ 253.00		£ 253.00		£ 3,036.00	£ -
23 Other exp...														
Rent/rates	£ 500.00		£ 500.00		£ 500.00		£ 500.00		£ 500.00		£ 500.00		£ 6,000.00	£ -
Heating/L...	£ 208.00		£ 208.00		£ 208.00		£ 208.00		£ 208.00		£ 208.00		£ 2,496.00	£ -
Insurance	£ 83.00		£ 83.00		£ 83.00		£ 83.00		£ 83.00		£ 83.00		£ 996.00	£ -
Repairs	£ 1,500.00		£ -		£ -		£ -		£ -		£ -		£ 3,000.00	£ -
Cleaning	£ 8.33		£ 8.33		£ 8.33		£ 8.33		£ 8.33		£ 8.33		£ 100.00	£ -
Telephone	£ 30.00		£ 30.00		£ 30.00		£ 30.00		£ 30.00		£ 30.00		£ 360.00	£ -
Prof. Fees	£ -		£ -		£ -		£ -		£ -		£ 200.00		£ 600.00	£ -
Depreciation	£ 415.00		£ 415.00		£ 415.00		£ 415.00		£ 415.00		£ 415.00		£ 4,980.00	£ -
25														
29 Finance...	£ 583.00		£ 583.00		£ 583.00		£ 583.00		£ 583.00		£ 583.00		£ 6,996.00	£ -
e Total fixed...	£ 3,580.33	£ -	£ 2,080.33	£ -	£ 2,080.33	£ -	£ 2,080.33	£ -	£ 2,080.33	£ -	£ 2,280.33	£ -	£28,564.00	£ -
f Net profit...	(£ 610.33)	£ -	£ 889.67	£ -	(£ 100.33)	£ -	(£ 100.33)	£ -	(£ 100.33)	£ -	£ 194.67	£ -	£20,936.00	£ -
g Sales you...	£ 6,148.05		£ 3,572.29		£ 3,572.29		£ 3,572.29		£ 3,572.29		£ 3,915.72		£49,049.29	

Table 2: THE CASHFLOW FORECAST

Month / Figures rounded to £s	April Budget	April Actual	May Budget	May Actual	June Budget	June Actual	July Budget	July Actual	August Budget	August Actual	September Budget	September Actual
Income												
1 Sales (including VAT) - Cash	£ 5,992.50	-	£ 5,992.50	-	£ 12,983.75	-	£ 17,977.50	-	£ 19,975.00	-	£ 7,990.00	-
2 — Debtors												
3 Other trading income												
4 Loans you have received												
5 New capital	£ 2,000.00											
6 Selling of assets												
7 Other receipts												
a Total receipts	£ 7,992.50	-	£ 5,992.50	-	£ 12,983.75	-	£ 17,977.50	-	£ 19,975.00	-	£ 7,990.00	-
Payments												
8 Cash for goods you have bought	£ 1,797.75	-	£ 1,797.75	-	£ 3,895.13	-	£ 5,393.25	-	£ 5,992.50	-	£ 2,397.00	-
9 Payments to creditors												
10 Owner or directors' withdrawals					£ 1,000.00	-	£ 1,000.00	-	£ 1,000.00	-	£ 1,000.00	-
11 Wages and Salaries (net)	£ 510.00	-	£ 510.00	-	£ 1,105.00	-	£ 1,530.00	-	£ 1,700.00	-	£ 680.00	-
12 PAYE/NI	£ 90.00	-	£ 90.00	-	£ 195.00	-	£ 270.00	-	£ 300.00	-	£ 120.00	-
13 Capital Items (eg equipment and vehicles)	£ 2,000.00											
14 Transport and Packaging												
15 Rent or rates	£ 1,000.00		£ 250.00		£ 250.00		£ 1,000.00		£ 250.00		£ 250.00	
16 Services			£ -		£ 800.00		£ -		£ -		£ 1,000.00	
17 Loan repayments	£ 583.00		£ 583.00		£ 583.00		£ 583.00		£ 583.00		£ 583.00	
18 Hire or leasing repayments												
19 Interest												
20 Bank or finance charges	£ 200.00		£ -		£ -		£ -		£ -		£ 200.00	
21 Professional fees												
22 Advertising												
23 Insurance	£ 83.00		£ 83.00		£ 83.00		£ 83.00		£ 83.00		£ 83.00	
24 Repairs	£ -		£ -		£ -		£ -		£ -		£ 1,500.00	
25 Other Expenses	£ 300.00		£ 300.00		£ 300.00		£ 300.00		£ 300.00		£ 300.00	
26 VAT							£ 2,603.00					
27 Corporation tax and so on												
28 Dividends												
b Total payments	£ 6,563.75	-	£ 3,613.75	-	£ 8,211.13	-	£ 12,762.25	-	£ 10,208.50	-	£ 8,113.00	-
c Net cashflow (a - b)	£ 1,428.75	-	£ 2,378.75	-	£ 4,772.63	-	£ 5,215.25	-	£ 9,766.50	-	(£ 123.00)	-
29 Opening bank balance	£ -		£ 1,428.75		£ 3,807.50		£ 8,580.13		£ 13,795.38		£ 23,561.88	
d Closing bank balance (C +/- Line 29)	£ 1,428.75	£ 1,428.75	£ 3,807.50	£ 3,807.50	£ 8,580.13	£ 8,580.13	£ 13,795.38	£ 13,795.38	£ 23,561.88	£ 23,561.88	£ 23,438.88	£ 23,438.88

Figures rounded to £s	October Budget	October Actual	November Budget	November Actual	December Budget	December Actual	January Budget	January Actual	February Budget	February Actual	March Budget	March Actual	Total Budget	Total Actual
Receipts														
1 Sales...-Cash	£ 5,992.50	£ -	£ 5,992.50	£ -	£ 3,995.00	£ -	£ 3,995.00	£ -	£ 3,995.00	£ -	£ 4,993.75	£ -	£ 99,875.00	£ -
2 ... -Debtors														£ -
3 Other trad...														£ -
4 Loans...														£ -
5 New cap...													£ 2,000.00	£ -
6 Selling of...														£ -
7 Other rec...														£ -
a Total rec...	£ 5,992.50	£ -	£ 5,992.50	£ -	£ 3,995.00	£ -	£ 3,995.00	£ -	£ 3,995.00	£ -	£ 4,993.75	£ -	£101,875.00	£ -
Payments														
8 Cash for...	£ 1,797.75	£ -	£ 1,797.75	£ -	£ 1,198.50	£ -	£ 1,198.50	£ -	£ 1,198.50	£ -	£ 1,498.13	£ -	£ 29,962.50	£ -
9 Pay..cred...													£ -	£ -
10 Owner...	£ 1,000.00		£ 1,000.00		£ 1,000.00		£ 1,000.00		£ 1,000.00		£ 1,000.00		£10,000.00	£ -
11 Wages...	£ 510.00		£ 510.00		£ 340.00		£ 340.00		£ 340.00		£ 425.00		£ 8,500.00	£ -
12 PAYE/NI	£ 90.00	£ -	£ 90.00	£ -	£ 60.00	£ -	£ 60.00	£ -	£ 60.00		£ 75.00	£ -	£ 1,500.00	£ -
13 Capital It...													£ 2,000.00	£ -
14 Transport...														£ -
15 Rent or rates	£ 1,000.00		£ 250.00		£ 250.00		£ 1,000.00		£ 250.00		£ 250.00		£ 6,000.00	£ -
16 Services	£ -		£ -		£ 350.00		£ -		£ -		£ 350.00		£ 2,500.00	£ -
17 Loan repay...	£ 583.00		£ 583.00		£ 583.00		£ 583.00		£ 583.00		£ 583.00		£ 6,996.00	£ -
18 Hire or leas...														£ -
19 Interest														£ -
20 Bank or fin...								£ -		£ -				£ -
21 Prof. fees	£ -		£ -		£ -		£ -				£ 200.00		£ 600.00	£ -
22 Advertising														£ -
23 Insurance	£ 83.00		£ 83.00		£ 83.00		£ 83.00		£ 83.00		£ 83.00		£ 996.00	£ -
24 Repairs	£ -		£ -		£ -		£ -		£ -		£ 1,500.00		£ 3,000.00	£ -
25 Other Exp...	£ 300.00		£ 300.00		£ 300.00		£ 300.00		£ 300.00		£ 300.00		£ 3,600.00	£ -
26 VAT	£ 4,790.00						£ 1,666.00						£ 9,059.00	£ -
27 Corp tax...							£ 4,000.00						£ 4,000.00	£ -
28 Dividends														£ -
b Total pay...	£ 10,153.75	£ -	£ 4,613.75	£ -	£ 4,164.50	£ -	£ 10,230.50	£ -	£ 3,814.50	£ -	£ 6,264.13	£ -	£ 88,713.50	£ -
c Net cashfl...	(£ 4,161.25)	£ -	£ 1,378.75	£ -	(£ 169.50)	£ -	(£ 6,235.50)	£ -	£ 180.50	£ -	(£ 1,270.38)	£ -	£ 13,161.50	£ -
29 Opening bal...	£23,438.88	£19,277.63	£19,277.63	£20,656.38	£20,656.38	£20,486.88	£20,486.88	£14,251.38	£14,251.38	£14,431.88	£14,431.88	£13,161.50	£ 13,161.50	£26,323.00
d Closing bal...	£19,277.63	£19,277.63	£20,656.38	£20,656.38	£20,486.88	£20,486.88	£14,251.38	£14,251.38	£14,431.88	£14,431.88	£13,161.50	£13,161.50	£26,323.00	£26,323.00

The layout shown shown in the tables is not untypical of the types of reports the banks might wish to see. When compiling such a report it may be necessary to include more or less detail but in any case, adopting such an approach to the Practice affairs at the beginning of the financial year may well prove to be beneficial if objectives are achieved. The figures contained in the tables are shown purely for illustration and are not based on factual information.

Avoiding the Overdraft

Adopting the above principles will go a long way to ensuring the Practice meets its objectives and therefore avoids the telephone call from the bank and the invitation to meet the manager. There are early warning signs that can be identified and corrected if appropriate prompt action is taken. These are as follows:

- Payment of large bills before full reimbursement has been received

- Delayed reimbursements

- Excessive drawings by doctors

- Payment of partnership or doctors tax, when no reserve has been created.

When the doctors take money from the Practice as drawings, it is in anticipation of their annual profits. Unlike PAYE staff who have their tax and National Insurance accounted for at the time the payment is made, Sole Traders and Partnerships taxpayers pay tax and NI at a later deferred time. The obvious danger is that if no contingency is created for future tax liabilities, it can create a false sense of security at the bank and funds may be inadvertently spent frugally on expenditure that otherwise might not have been incurred if this money was not available. The other danger is that it is possible for partners' capital accounts to become heavily overdrawn and this has the result of reducing the net worth of the doctor on the balance sheet. With the most recent reforms and the fact that there are more and more things that can be claimed by achieving targets and efficiency, it is vitally important that items are claimed in the most appropriate quarter or period. It is also important that partners' drawings are regularly reviewed (say quarterly or even monthly) in line with predicted forecasts and then adjusted accordingly. PMS Contracts should make this process easier, because a contract value is agreed at the beginning of the year. To avoid dispute, Practice policy can be defined and if appropriate written into the Partnership Agreement.

The two key areas to concentrate on to improve cashflow are:

1) Do focus on list size queries and, in particular, 'ghost' patients. In a Primary Care led NHS that is driven more and more by proven list size and capitation-based models, each patient registered with the Practice is guaranteeing a secure level of income

2) Whenever target payments are involved, make sure that you do not exceed the maximum that you are allowed to claim in any one period. There is no point doing the extra work if the end result is not reimbursable. Also the way the reimbursement system works means that, in many cases, once upper targets are reached, any excess is not reimbursable or may attract a lower level of reimbursement. Under PMS or the new Contract, there may not be the need to achieve a higher level of work to obtain the same level of return. Profitability can also be achieved by doctors working less hours, ie: a return in time spent rather than money.

Remember that, whoever is responsible for the overall cashflow management of the Practice, the overall liquidity of the Practice is the sole responsibility of the practitioner or partners. Sensible decisions taken today will ensure that the General Practitioner can retire when he or she plans and not be trapped into working more years than envisaged because of poor cash management.

CHAPTER 4

THE NEW GMS CONTRACT

At the time of writing, details concerning the new GMS Contract remain to a degree speculative, although it must be said the principles have been laid down and many organisations are beginning to comment on how the contract might work. It must not be forgotten that many practices have already decided to elect to sign up to PMS Contracts. The PMS Contracts are currently accepting their fifth wave of entries and this is something of an anomaly, given that PMS originally started as a pilot scheme, to be evaluated after three years. In most cases, PMS Contracts have been rolled over. It is important that both PMS and existing GMS practices understand the window of opportunity that the new GMS Contract might offer. The new Contract was due to be rolled out in April 2003, however, while the speed of introduction will be determined by local factors, it will be governed centrally by new primary enabling legislation.

The new GMS Contract will include a nationally negotiated framework, detailing services to be delivered across the country. It is expected that the new Contract will be adopted by all PCTs. One of the main principles behind the new Contract is that overall performance by the Practice should now be linked to financial incentives. The Contract is designed to allow PCTs to ensure that patients can be guaranteed access to a minimum of existing services. In certain medical specialties, all practices will be expected to deliver services; in others some practices may elect to carry out certain services and not others. The Government's investment in NHS resources is meant to allow the positive development of a much wider range of contract services. Another intention of the new Contract is to ensure that the GP (and his or her medical practice team) keep workloads within acceptable limits.

What's in It for the Practice ?

The new GMS Contract will provide the funding to allow a practice to deliver Primary Care services to its patients. The allocation will be set by means of a national formula designed to ensure that the "money follows the patient." The basic concept is that there will be a global sum, which will be distributed using a national formula based on Practice list size. Therefore each patient will have a basic worth to the Practice. New ways of working should allow a greater degree of flexibility in respect of the working patterns of the Practice, which will help to alleviate some recruitment and retention problems. The Contract will recognize that the GP's time is a finite resource and will allow the GP to earn a reasonable sum for a reasonable input of time.

The new Contract is designed to be more flexible and have built-in incentives, also allowing easier ways for GPs to change the way that they work. Under the old rules or under a PMS Contract, GPs were expected to provide defined core services. In the case of the new Contract, core services may vary between practices with patients being cross-referred between practices. This is being expedited by the way the patient list will be pooled under the Practice not the individual doctor. The idea behind the Contract is to continue to provide quality services to patients but with the option of improving the working conditions of the primary medical team. The Practice will be able to use the GMS allocation in a variety of ways. Time will be protected for continuing professional education and individuals will be able to ensure that there is appropriate career development. This should help in areas where there are still recruitment and retention problems.

The intention is to develop more exciting career opportunities for all GPs and Practice staff. Much of the current bureaucracy will also be removed, to enable GPs and the their teams to become more supportive of each other.

The new GMS Contract is intended to promote equality and incentives for all. Additionally, by promoting a more friendly practice and making working practices more flexible, it is also expected that GPs can properly plan for retirement, safe in the knowledge that they will receive a fair return for their pension contributions.

How Will It Benefit PCTs?

The new GMS Contract is designed to promote co-operation between different GP practices, and between practices and the PCT. It also encourages improved communication and co-ordination between practices, the PCTs and other service providers, secondary care and other organisations such as the social services. The framework of the new Contract will give PCTs the necessary funds to provide and promote the delivery of quality Primary Care services to their demographic population. These funds and the way they are allocated will mean that services can be identified and organised in a way that better serves the needs of the local population. New initiatives and primary care developments can then be funded by PCTs from the overall allocation. Practices will be expected to provide immediately necessary treatments and emergency services. Temporary residents will also be seen as they are now. PCTs will fund these areas globally using past treatment records as a basis for calculating the funding. Where there are larger numbers of temporary residents due to local factors, special arrangements will be put in place. PCTs will also be able to extend the use of Primary Care facilities to take into account the access needs of the local working population, for example: by offering surgeries outside normal working hours.

Funding under the New Contract

Unlike the existing Contracts which applied to individual GPs, the new GMS Contract will be between the local Primary Care Trust and, subject to legislation, the Practice (be it a sole GP, a multi-handed practice or a group of practices). Individual GP patient lists will cease and there will be a pooled list for the Practice.

Funding for the new GMS Contract will follow the patient. The aim is to introduce a national methodology where the allocation of resources will be linked to the number of patients. The funding will allow room for national and local flexibility. In short it will become a budget model and effectively cash-limit resources. Previously, areas on non-cash-limited funding would be paid irrespective of cost. Under the new Contract, such areas will be paid according to a formula, which is unlikely to offer the same flexibility of a non-cash-limited sum of money.

A new formula will be used to calculate the relative amount of the national sum available to practices to deliver a basic range of essential and additional primary care services. The provision of the overall sum will provide practices with greater flexibility than they have at present to organise the delivery of patient care in a way that meets the needs of their patients. At the same time, it allows GPs and practice staff flexibility about their own individual working patterns. The PCT will manage a number of budgets both through the unified allocation and through a nationally determined proportion of the overall sum. Not all practices will provide the same services. Indeed, the PCT can be responsible for the provision of such services. There will be a definition of essential services that must be provided together with a description of those services that will be regarded as additional. Full guidance and enabling legislation is still awaited for this.

Quality and Outcomes Framework

The services delivered by the Practice will be via a graded framework of levels that encourages and rewards movement to the highest level, particularly facilitating improvements in those practices that are struggling to keep above the minimum standards. Practices will agree with the PCT which level they expect to achieve before the beginning of each year. The Practice will have to demonstrate its ability to deliver a particular level if it wishes to enter at anything other than minimum levels. It will receive a form of indicative payment appropriate to that level which will support the proposed quality standards for that year including, where necessary, any costs not already properly funded through the overall sum. The payments will be made on a regular basis either monthly or quarterly, but there may be exceptional cases where the full indicative payment is required in a lump sum. At the end of the contract year the Practice will receive an attainment payment if it has achieved the agreed standards.

Those practices entering at the minimum level will be expected to work through each of the levels demonstrating continuous improvement. The majority of the framework will include national standards but will also allow for a range of clinical standards. The Practice will deliver certain core services, on top of which they will deliver certain specific services. These additional services might be different from those offered by another practice on the same level. There will be a detailed methodology by which PCTs will be able to assess practices through evaluation on an annual basis (or more frequently where necessary). This will be a self-assessment style evaluation underpinned by the principle that practices would not be subject to unnecessary bureaucracy. All practices would need to provide appropriate documentary evidence by means of an agreed annual statement or return – a similar process to filling in your tax return! And, in just the same way as the Inland Revenue undertakes random inspections of tax returns, visits will be undertaken to check that Practice returns are accurate. Each visit would include a comprehensive review and discussion with all clinicians and the Practice Manager. It will be essential to ensure that the visit avoids disruption to the patients or other members of the Practice. Practices would be adequately supported for participating in the review process. Consideration is being given ensuring that an appeal process is put in place to protect the interests of practices.

Premises

The provision of necessary practice premises requires that GPs incur significant cost liabilities but PCT and LIFT funding schemes do exist to help practices with the cost of premises, however, there only is enough funding to allow a limited number of plans to be progressed at any given time. More and more private funding is being targeted. These schemes allow private money and investors to build new premises and then to act as landlords by leasing these newly developed premises back to the GPs by means of legally binding agreements.

The funding for new premises should provide a range of support to all GPs within the new Contract. There will be national methodologies to ensure that the appropriate risk factors and revenue consequences can be evaluated, allowing the highest potential return for GPs. One of the problems with property investment is calculating the actual return on capital invested. Demographic position is a major factor in deciding whether a property investment will yield a positive return. The new GMS Contract will allow monies to be invested in all areas, with GPs being given access to different investment routes, of course ensuring that there is parity in the way that funds are distributed. PCTs will, of course, be responsible for ensuring that any premises schemes represent value for money and are in the general interests to the patients.

There will be further provisions introduced that could make funding available for GPs who find themselves in negative equity situations. Such funding would be a massive incentive to allow GPs to move from sub-standard premises and enter agreements to move into new, purpose-built premises. Some of the possibilities that may be considered are things like mortgage redemption costs, allowing PCTs to take up options on land purchase. However, existing arrangements for cost rent payments will continue and PCTs will be able to review cost rent payments when practices look towards remortgaging. Where the private sector is involved, funding will become available for paying for legal and professional costs.

Arrangements will be put in place for practices that are modernised or extended. Under these arrangements the Practice will pay notional rent in addition to cost rent and there will be abatement on GP capital invested. Leaseholder GPs who improve their premises will receive a payment of notional rent. The timescale for repayment of such grants will be extended to 10 years for owner-occupiers and 15 years for those who rent their premises. PCTs will be allowed to reimburse service charges directly. They will introduce reviews of building cost factors and introduce index-linked leases. PCTs will have more say when it comes to negotiating with third party contracts. This may include the provision for assignment of leases to the PCT in the event that a departing GP is unable to do this. There is no question that significant investment in Primary Care premises from Government, private finance and GPs themselves is currently needed – not only to provide appropriate standards, but also to ensure that the current targets and standards can be met. Funds will be identified for investment in those areas that need the most improvement. This is nothing new, but the new Contract is aiming to provide both the PCTs and the practices more flexibility. The allocations that PCTs receive will be sufficient to support both capital and revenue costs. This could mean that a practice could be reimbursed for more costly items of capital equipment, (for example, clinical equipment to be used in the delivery of new services in the Primary Care setting).

The Use of Information Technology

In the past, practices would receive a level of reimbursement towards computer purchases. This aspect will be removed under the new Contract. PCTs will receive the funding for the purchase and procurement of such items. This will be extended to include the running costs and maintenance of such systems and will also include integrated sites as well as landlines and wireless LANs between practices, PCTs and even hospitals. Although the PCT will have control of the finances, practices will still be able to choose a preferred system from a number of accredited suppliers. There will be those who remember that the same principal was adopted when fundholding was introduced. Let's hope that, whatever Primary Care systems are used, that they are allowed to continue for long enough to justify the investment in time and money that their introduction incurred. The principal behind fundholding systems was quite robust, providing specific financial and clinical data. Servers will normally be located within practices, however it could be appropriate in certain circumstances to have such facilities hosted elsewhere. How does this involve the new Contract? Quite simply, those practices that subscribe to the information technology strategy of the PCT will have incentives built into their Contract to use such services to control their overall workload.

Practice Management

Good practice management can encourage best practice, make the Practice more profitable and benefit the clinical staff as well. It is recognised that good management in General Practice is a contributing factor to how effective a practice is overall. To that end the new Contract will allow incentives to be built in that promote the expansion of the role of practice management. This will include the skills and expertise needed to deliver the management function. Within the overall sum, management costs will be funded at 100%. Again, this is another concept adopted from the fundholding management scheme.

Practices will have a say about how their management funding can be used. Of course, many practices will employ a full-time Practice Manager, but where smaller practices only employ a part-time manager it will possible for a practice to share a manager with one or more other practices. There is a suggestion that PCTs could provide this management expertise but, of course, this could result in a potential conflict of interest. There are a number of Primary Care specialist professionals (such as management consultants, specialist accountants and former PCT employees) who can be instrumental in helping practices to make the most of the potential practice management incentives offered under the new Contract. Indeed, wise practice managers should be already evaluating and comparing the cost benefits of the PMS Contracts and the new GMS Contract. Not surprisingly, management competence will become an important issue under the new Contract. A good starting point for a practice management role would be to have some form of financial qualification because funding issues have become so important in Primary Care. Running a practice effectively and with a sound understanding of financial issues will mean that the Practice will achieve a greater level of profitability.

The GP's Career

Some might say that being a GP is one of the most secure professions financially. This is partly due to the fact that upon achieving parity in a practice, there is little or no uncertainty about achieving an income. Nonetheless, it is true that income levels and workload patterns can vary.

The new Contract takes a triple-layered approach to the structure of a GP's career:

1. It addresses the needs of new and returning GPs who may need additional experience in some medical areas. The new Contract offers opportunities for gaining that experience – sometimes through the creation of salaried positions that allow the GP to work across a range of GP practices.

2. It encourages GPs who have additional skills (clinical or non-clinical) to provide those services to the local Hospital Trusts or PCT under a new style of Contract that uses the "plus option" where a GP might provide a secondary service such as colposcopy.

3. It provides incentives for senior GPs to take on leadership roles such as training, mentorship, Local Medical Committees and board appointments at PCT level.

The Contract will allow GPs to opt for each or all of the different layers at different times throughout their career.

Salaried Option

Under the new GMS Contract, GPs will be allowed to adopt the salaried role. Many are seeing this as being an attractive option if the approach and the terms and conditions are acceptable. It is likely that these conditions will reflect national standards and may reflect salary levels as recommended by the Doctor and Dentist Review Board (DDRB). In addition to the salary, there will be centrally controlled funds for GP and staff development. These funds will be controlled by the PCT.

Seniority Payments

Because of the complexities caused by the new working arrangements, it has been suggested that the transition to the new style Contract will be flexible enough to take into account existing Seniority Payments but there will be no provision for new Seniority Payments. This will mean that those GPs who already receive Seniority Payments will not be disadvantaged by the change, however, it does mean that new GPs entering the profession will find that such payments will disappear.

Appraisal

Arrangements for appraisal under the new Contract have already been agreed and these will be extended to cover both PMS and GMS contracts. The appraisal arrangements for Scotland will be slightly different from those in England and Wales but appraisals will probably all follow a designated form.

Childcare

PCTs will be responsible for ensuring that adequate provision or access to economical childcare is available in each practice. The aim is to allow more flexible working arrangements for GPs and the Practice staff as well as helping the Practice to maintain (or extend) its opening hours. The idea is to allow those in Primary Care to share the similar level of childcare provision enjoyed in other areas of the NHS.

Pensions

The issue of pensions is still being heavily debated. Negotiations are still ongoing between representative organisations and government but agreement has yet to be reached about a number of issues. It is hoped that the new Contract will ensure pension provisions that will both improve GP morale and improve potential retention of GPs within the service. It is hoped is that the pensionable pay is set at the highest possible level. At the moment, certain parts of a GP's pay are non-pensionable and therefore separate arrangements must be made for taking tax advantages on these earnings. The ultimate issue that needs to be considered here is the status of the GP. Becoming a salaried individual will potentially change the tax status of the GP. Currently GPs fall under the self-assessment system, but becoming a salaried GP under the PAYE system will mean that a GP would lose certain tax advantages as he or she would no longer be able to claim for certain items.

Community Hospitals, Minor Injury Services and Immediate Care

Community Hospitals (previously known as Cottage Hospitals) offer a large amount of intermediate care and undertake a significant amount of minor injury services. The minor injury treatment in these hospitals is often provided by GPs – sometimes actually in the local Community

Hospital but often at the local GP Practice. Community Hospitals do not have contracted resident staff and the first point of contact is normally a GP or a local practice because, in some locations, particularly rural areas, the local General Hospital (and its A&E Department) may be many miles away.

Under the new Contract, GPs in remote areas may also provide an agreed level of support to the ambulance and emergency rescue services. It is vital to ensure that emergencies receive very rapid responses and, so, the new Contract recognises that GPs often provide emergency services outside normal practice hours and at all sorts of locations. It is obvious that this type of service needs adequate training and resources for specialist equipment. It is also felt that there should also be a clear incentive to GPs to provide such services.

In recognition of the fact that local GP practices are an integral part of the way in which local Community Hospital services are delivered in many parts of the UK, GPs who provide such services may qualify for special funding under the new Contract. The new Contract may also examine ways in which the role of the GP can be regarded as being akin to work undertaken by clinical assistants or hospital practitioners.

The New GMS Contract Levels

Under the new Contract, practices will be expected to achieve particular "levels" of service. PMS pilot contracts already provide measurement and quality criteria within their contracts. It is expected that the new GMS Contract will follow a similar model.

In order to explain and illustrate the proposed levels of service, we have taken the example of the treatment targets for ischaemic heart disease. (A similar approach will be adopted for other national disease targets):

Level 1 (Entry Level)

Practices who enter at the entry level will be expected to have an accurate and up-to-date register of patients recorded on a suitable computerised system. The details might include information pertaining to long term drugs and information about how often such patients have been reviewed.

Level 2

Level 2 includes all the criteria required for Level 1 plus a further eight quality standards would need to be attained:

Standard Measurement Criteria

- Patients will be reviewed or offered review at least annually (including a review of medication)

- Smoking, body mass index, exercise status and alcohol consumption will be recorded and appropriate advice offered

- Blood glucose will be measured in all patients (at least once following diagnosis) and treated where appropriate

- Blood pressure should be recorded at least annually

- All patients should be taking regular aspirin except where contra-indicated or not tolerated

- All patients with symptomatic coronary heart disease should have access to sublingual GTN

- All patients who require regular symptomatic treatment should be treated with a beta-blockers (unless contra-indicated or experiencing significant side-effects)

- Patients should have their blood lipids measured at least annually and prescribed a statin in line with national guidelines.

Each standard will have exception and exemption criteria. These criteria must be in place before the level can be attained. There would be an expectation of an improvement year-on-year in the outcome indicators with Level 2 payments continuing until the Practice has met all the Level 3 entry standards.

Level 3

To attain Level 3, the Practice will have already achieved Levels 1 and 2 and be able to demonstrate continuous improvement in their services. Patients would be selected to have their total cholesterol or LDL and blood pressure reduced in accordance with national guidance. The target is to see an improvement in 95% of those patients selected for cholesterol or LDL treatment and in 85% of those selected for antihypertensive treatment. Both target figures would be inclusive of exception reporting. A practice will need to demonstrate a continuous improvement in all targets before being accepted to Level 4.

Level 4

Level 4 is effectively an enhancement and continuation of Level 3. The Practice will need to demonstrate that the levels attained in Level 3 are now being consistently maintained and delivered.

Level 5 (Premium Level)

This level is achieved through the delivery of every standard to the highest possible level across three quality criteria:

- Clinical services – in all defined clinical aspects

- Organisational skills – both clinical and practice management organisational skills including interaction with other members of the primary health care team

- Patient perspective – ensuring that the patients are informed and can participate in shaping the delivery of services.

Quality Levels and Payments

Under the new GMS Contract, the Practice will not qualify for incremental increases in payments at Level 1 or at Level 4.

Level 2 increments will be available, but given at a slower rate than Level 3. Each step at each level will require higher target achievements and deliverables, however, achieving demonstrable improvements/targets/service requirements at Level 2 (and thus being eligible for increased payments) will be less arduous that achieving demonstrable improvements at Level 3.

Aspiration payments (which offer an incentive to the practices to successfully complete the Contract) will be the same in each level.

All the criteria for each level must be fulfilled before the Practice can move onto the next level. However after Level 4, higher attainment is achieved by consistent improvement of the services delivered.

The PMS Contract (or PMS Plus Contract) is based on a negotiated contract sum – the agreed amount of money that is payable to the Practice. This sum includes the baseline funding but also includes separate individual funding headings for additional services that the Practice offers or other items such as particular staff or drugs payments.

The new GMS Contract is a progressive funding mechanism. The way in which it operates will be determined firstly by enabling legislation and then, of course, there may be local factors as determined by the PCT, which will affect overall funding. The key word for either type of Contract is incentive. For a practice to establish which model is best for it, the Practice will need to evaluate the overall contract sum in both models. Then the astute Practice will apply its own financial model. If it manages this model, then it would be possible to generate the desired outcomes in either model. In simple terms it will be necessary to compare both financial sums in relation to the amount of work and time needed to generate that sum. Then this should be compared against the expenditure for running the Practice and the model that shows the greatest profit will be the preferred option.

The real truth about any GP contract will be the fact that the funding mechanism will be cash-limited and certainly controlled and influenced by the local PCT. As with all models or new schemes, windows of opportunity are normally available in the first years of operation. The reason is that after the first year, cash-limited funds will be more difficult to access. Given that these models are about cash-limited contract sums, it is likely that one of the models will be subsumed into the other to become the real new GMS Contract.

CHAPTER 5

MANAGEMENT COST AND APPORTIONMENT

Staffing the Practice

The new GMS Contract and the old PMS Contract permit staffing allocations to be used in a variety of ways. The new Contracts will allow an internal review of working practices, allowing staff to undertake new duties, which may be more financially beneficial. However, very often these staff do not know sufficient information to perform certain duties effectively. Information is the key and the correct use of information can produce staff efficiencies. Redeploying staff and prioritising roles can lead to cost reductions. One way of dealing with this is to treat the Practice like a small business and a going concern. The following items are things that can be reviewed and dealt with in house, ensuring that liabilities can be met on time and in the most cost-effective manner.

The Practice as an Employer

The responsibilities of employers have always been there, but the rules effective from 1996/97 have meant a further major reform for Practitioners. It may not affect any of your existing staff, but in the event that a member of staff is expected to file a self-assessment return, there are certain things of which the employer should be aware. Whereas in the past, employees could complete returns by stating 'as per attached PAYE records' or 'as per P11d', the self-assessment regulations now require specific amounts to be shown.

Staff and Self-Assessment

Since 1994, the Practitioner as an employer will have been aware of the self-assessment tax return system that requires that any employee who would be expected to complete a tax return must have access to information about PAYE, benefits in kind and expenses payments. Proposals were outlined to ensure that employers gave employees the correct information in sufficient time to allow them to fulfil their tax obligations. The legislation governing these changes (Statutory Instrument No.1284: 1995) came into effect on 6 April 1996.

The New Rules of the Game

Each year the employer must supply each employee with Form P60. This is a certificate that details all pay and tax deductions. In the past, there was no time limit on when this information is to be supplied. However for the tax year 1996/97 onwards, there is a requirement that each individual receives a P60 by the 31st May after the end of the tax year concerned.

New Deadline Date:
Issue P60s to all staff no later than 31 MAY 2003 for 2002/2003 tax year

As an employer, you will be free to decide how this information is provided to staff as long as the deadline date is met.

Another familiar form, the P45, has undergone certain changes. The reason for this is that the self-assessment forms require employees to enter figures for pay and tax from each employment. The staff that are likely to be affected by this are new employees or those staff who work for more than one general practice. Normally, the employee will rely on Form P60 for tax and pay details, but this form will not necessarily give details where there has been a change to employment or a break in the cumulative operation of PAYE. To account for these circumstances, a new four part P45 was introduced in April 1996. Part 1a of the new-style P45 is completed for retention by the employee. Therefore, as an employer, the new four-part form will need to be completed with part 1 being sent to the Tax Office and parts 1a, 2 and 3 being given to the employee. The employee should retain part 1a for his or her records and parts 2 and 3 should be given to the new employer.

New Form P45:
With effect from 6 APRIL 1996, any member of staff
leaving the Practice will need to be supplied with
parts 1a, 2 and 3 of the new four-part P45

There are slight changes to the type of information detailed on the form. The employer will complete the form and include details of the following:

• For cumulative tax codes – details of cumulative tax and pay

• Details of tax and pay for 'this employment'

In the event that the two sets of figures above are the same, the employer may enter only the cumulative amount.

Although it is not likely to affect many employees, there are a growing number of practices where staff do receive benefits in kind or expenses payments. Benefits in kind and/or expenses payments must be accounted for on Form P11d and submitted to the Inland Revenue by the employer. Previously, the deadline for sending forms P11d to the Inland Revenue was the 6 June. With effect from the tax year 1996/97, this deadline has been extended to 6 July.

New Deadline Date:
Form P11d to be submitted to the Inland Revenue
no later than 6 JULY 2003

Previously as an employer there was only a requirement to send Form P11d information to the Inland Revenue. Very often this caused problems where differing information was submitted on the P11d and supplied in a tax return. Since the year 1996/97 it has been a requirement that exactly the same information will need to be supplied to the employee as is detailed on the Form P11d sent to the Revenue. Therefore, for all employees still in employment at the end of the tax year, the employer must automatically supply these details. For employees who have left employment between 5 April and 6 July, details must be sent to the last known address. However, for all other employees who left during the tax year concerned, there is no obligation on the employer to provide this information unless they are requested to do so.

Written Request for P11d Information:

Where the Practice receives a WRITTEN request for this information from a former employee, it must be supplied (subject to the request being received within THREE YEARS of the relevant tax year)

The employer is free to elect how he or she wishes to supply the P11d information to the employee, whether as a photocopy of the original form or some other form of agreed substitute. With increasing computerisation of General Practice, more and more practices are turning to the use of computerised payroll packages, which in general provide approved substitutes of key payroll forms.

Key Deadline Date:

For those former employees who request information within the three year time limit, the appropriate information must be returned no later than 30 DAYS after the written request

Whilst all the above may seem like minor administrative adjustments to existing practices, adopting good practice early on will ensure that the Practice does not spend valuable time at a later date trying to retrieve information that has been filed or stored away. By establishing a procedure whereby the P45 and P11d information is automatically supplied as part of the leaving routine, this will ensure that this particular obligation is fulfilled and therefore potentially valuable staff time is not wasted in the future.

Again the information entered on the Form P11d is slightly different from the normal P11 form. Where a benefit in kind is included, it is a requirement to show a cash equivalent on the P11d form. This represents the amount that is deemed to be taxable for each benefit, before any deductions for expenses, which may be claimed by the employee. There are changes that affect business entertainment and the operation of fixed car profit schemes, but these will not generally apply to Practice staff. However, if there is any doubt, employees should seek clarification from the employer who, in turn, should seek advice from his or her professional tax advisor.

To calculate the cash equivalent of benefits in kind:

- Ascertain the cost incurred and

- Subtract any amount made where an employee may have contributed towards the cost.

Where to Get Help

The wise Practice will look at what is currently available and make best use of a free resource. The Inland Revenue do provide an education and assistance programme for employers. The Practice should make best use of this opportunity whilst it exists as it could be withdrawn in the future. For more information about any of the above issues, the Practice should contact its local tax office to find out if any seminars are being run in the area. Also the Practice might wish to obtain up-to-date written guidance from the local tax office. Whatever the query, a simple telephone call to the local tax office can be a quick solution to obtaining the information required.

Penalties Relating to P11d Forms

All the above seems relatively straight forward, but there is a sting in the tail for those unaware of the changes. Under the new rules, the Inland Revenue can impose penalties if P11d information is not supplied but the Revenue will continue to ask the employer for a suitable explanation for incomplete or incorrect completion of Form P11d before imposing any penalty. In most events the Revenue will not follow up many P11d penalties, preferring instead to settle for voluntary settlements for tax and National Insurance Contributions due. In the event that penalty action is taken, the Practice has a right to appeal against the decision. However, the Practice should be warned that a penalty would only be overturned if there has been a genuine mistake made in good faith.

The correctly completed P11ds need to be sent to Inland Revenue by 6 July from 1996/97 onwards. This information will also need to be provided to the employee. Where information is not sent to the Revenue, the Revenue will remind the employer of its obligations and will encourage compliance with the requirements. Where the employer continues not to comply or the amounts involved are significant, the Revenue will pursue penalties rigorously. The new rules are designed to make employers give the employees the necessary information to complete their personal tax returns. Therefore there should be no need for the Revenue to take action against the employer unless the employee reports that the information has not been made available to them. The same course of action is applicable to the completion of Form P60. The seeking of penalties will be seen as being the last resort for persistent failure to comply, but if penalties are sought they can be an expensive mistake.

If a practice were to supply knowingly incorrect or incomplete information, the enabling legislation (Section 98(2) of the *Taxes Management Act* 1970) provides for a maximum penalty of £3,000 for each incorrect or incomplete P11d. It follows that the penalty is designed to cover a number of realities and therefore the maximum penalty will only be used in extreme or exceptional cases. Where it is a matter of negligence a much lower penalty would apply. The point to note is that these forms should not be completed in a hurry or pushed to one side, because all penalties of this nature are unnecessary and completely avoidable. Likewise where a practice fails to provide certain information, the possible penalties can be up to £300 per form imposed by the General or Special Commissioners and a further penalty of up to £60 per form which can be sought by the Revenue for each day that the failure continues.

Obviously the above are the severest penalties to be faced in the most extreme of cases, but any penalty or voluntary settlement should be avoidable and a small amount of time spent prior to the end of year in reviewing practice procedures should ensure that all the relevant work is completed accurately and on time.

Payroll Management

Introduction

It is vitally important the Practice payroll is managed by someone who is fully conversant with the technicalities of the Pay As You Earn (PAYE) system. The Practice should be aware that the Inland Revenue can select any practice at random for a PAYE review. Although routine in their nature, such a review may lead to a formal investigation, if there are irregularities identified, no matter the nature and however innocent the discoveries. This type of review could lead to the collection of unpaid tax, interest and penalty payments for up to the six previous years. It is imperative that this area of General Practice finance is not taken lightly as it represents a large percentage of the Practice expenditure. Areas commonly addressed by the Inland Revenue include:

- Petty cash payments to individuals
- Christmas gifts
- Christmas bonuses
- General bonuses or performance-related pay
- Part-time staff not eligible for tax or National Insurance
- Casual staff

- Contract staff performing routine work, for example secretarial tasks
- Benefits to staff, particularly for trainee GPs or salaried GPs
- Spouses' earnings

The above list is just an indication of the more frequently assessed areas and this is on top of reviewing the actual operation of the PAYE system itself.

How the PAYE System Works

The principle of the PAYE system is that taxation and National Insurance Contributions are paid at the same time as the employee is paid his or her salary, thereby ensuring that all taxation due is collected promptly. It is a requirement of regulations that the employer keeps records of both the pay and the deductions made. The amount calculated as being due to the Inland Revenue must be paid to the Collector of Taxes by the due date at the end of each month and a return detailing all the payments made and deductions must be made by a due date each year. Very often the payroll function is completed by a member of staff, who may inadvertently omit any part of the process, but even though this individual may have caused an error, it is the employer who is legally responsible and therefore becomes liable.

National Insurance Contributions (Class 1 NIC)

For some individuals who earn below a certain level (for 2002/03 it is weekly earnings less than £75.00), there is no requirement to pay National Insurance (NI). When this weekly amount is exceeded, then contributions become payable on the whole amount subject to an overall maximum per employee. The maximum is referred to as the Upper Earnings Limit (for 2002/03 the maximum weekly contribution is £49.60). Any earnings that exceed the Upper Earnings Limit will not be subject to further employees' contributions. However, employers' contributions are payable on all earnings including those above the Upper Earnings Limit.

When considering the cost of a member of staff, the employer should calculate the cost by adding on a figure of 13% to account for the employers' NI contributions.

Taxation of PAYE employees (Income Tax: Schedule E)

GPs are assessed for income tax on the majority of their income under Schedule D (which applies to sole traders and partnerships). However, employees are assessed under the PAYE system, which falls into the area of Schedule E. Unlike NI contributions, PAYE limits are not always so easy to understand. The reason for this is that each employee is entitled to personal allowances, but each employee may also have differing circumstances that may effect the overall allowances available to them.

The Inland Revenue informs employers of their employees' tax codes through the use of notice forms (Form P2). Incorrect use of these codes or their application at the wrong time will lead to unnecessary over- or underpayment of tax. If a new employee only has a Week 1 or Month 1 temporary tax code, then the tax calculated will be based purely on that one week's or one month's earnings only. Whilst the allowances given are often the full amount, this code restriction is known as an Emergency Tax Code. Most employees will receive a Cumulative Tax Code, which means that the tax payable is calculated on all earnings to date from the beginning of the tax year concerned. In other words, if an employee is above their allowance threshold, the additional money that they earn will continue to be taxed at source at the rates applicable at the time. Conversely, if an employee receives no pay or reduced pay in a given month causing the employee's cumulative earnings to fall below the allowable threshold, then a tax rebate becomes due.

Details of the current rates and tax tables are available free to employers from the local DSS offices and Inland Revenue offices. Most existing practices will automatically receive these tables as a matter of course.

The PAYE Responsibilities of the Practice

In General Practice, the doctors (as responsible employers) have a duty to operate the PAYE system and it should be borne in mind that if the employer fails to operate the system correctly, the tax due is still payable to the Collector of Taxes. Therefore, if you fail to account for payroll PAYE correctly at the time when the employees are paid (or if you are subsequently reviewed and informed that there are errors in the payroll), it is the employer, ie: the doctors, who must pay any tax liability. This leads to the added problem of trying to reclaim tax from the employees (which can be particularly difficult if the employee no longer works at the Practice). Do bear in mind that some reviews go back a full six years. A simple mistake could lead to longer-term problems. Irrespective of whose fault it is, the Inland Revenue is entitled to apply penalties and interest and these too would become the liability of the Practice. Whether operating a manual system or computerised payroll, always ensure that some form of random review is being carried out to ensure that the appropriate tables and codes are being used.

At the end of each month, there is a requirement to pay both the NI and tax to the Collector of Taxes. Each tax month is actually deemed as finishing on the 5th of a month with the tax due being payable within 14 days (ie: by the 19th of each month). There is also a requirement for employers to keep records for a minimum of three years. Do not forget that both the DSS and the Inland Revenue can ask to inspect your records at any time and you are not allowed to prevent them. Therefore there are three key times to check your payroll records:

- At the time the payroll is processed and payments made to employees
- At the time income tax and NI contributions are made to the Collector of Taxes
- At the end of each tax year

Paying your Staff

Whenever an employee is paid a salary or any form of remuneration, the Practice must consider the tax implications of the transaction by using the appropriate tax tables (previously referred to above) and calculating the correct amount of tax due. It must not be forgotten that the employee also has the right to use the appropriate tables to determine whether the payroll calculations are correct. If the Practice is using payroll software, it is important to check that the parameters (eg: the tax tables) being used correspond with those applicable to the current financial year. Remember that if you do not update your system the wrong percentages and allowances will be used and may cause you problems in the future.

Keeping Records

It is normal that payroll records are kept using Inland Revenue Form P11 (also known as the Deductions Working Sheet) or, in the case of computerised systems, an accepted alternative (which should normally approved by the Inland Revenue).

If you use a manual payroll system, then it is appropriate to use the Inland Revenue Form P11 (1996). The simple reason for this is that it is fully accepted by the Revenue and has been tried and tested for many years. Providing that you understand the various columns on the Form (see below) it will become relatively easy to audit the payroll.

For computerised records, it is allowable to use P11 substitutes, but if you do use substitute documentation it must include the minimum data specified in Form P11. These records must be kept for a minimum of three years and you do not have to send this information to the Inspector of Taxes.

When using the Inland Revenue Form P11 – the Deductions Working Sheet – each separate sheet will relate to an individual employee and consists of a number of columns, each of which provides specific information:

Column 1a

This is the earnings figure on which the employee's NIC is payable, ie: the amount of earnings that are liable to NI. Obviously if the earnings are below the lower limit, this amount will be nil. This will also be true for employees who are exempt. The total earnings figure will represent the amount between the lower and the upper limit. Where the upper limit is exceeded, the maximum figure should be entered.

Column 1b

This is the total of both the employee's and employer's NI contribution.

Column 1c

This represents the employee's share of the NIC only.

Column 1d

Earnings on which employee's contributions at contracted-out rates are payable. For employees paying D and E rate contributions and as members of a pension scheme, this should represent the part of their earnings above the lower earnings limit, but below the upper earning limits as defined within the NIC tables. For other employees the amount will be nil.

Column 1e

Employee's contribution at contracted-out rate. The portion is shown in the NIC tables and is included in the amount shown in Column 1c.

Column 1f

The amount of statutory sick pay including the total pay for the week or month (as included in column 2).

Column 1g

The amount of statutory maternity pay recovered in the period.

Column 2

This represents the total pay in the period including any statutory sick pay or maternity pay.

Column 3

This represents the total pay to date and is a cumulative value.

Column 4a

This figure is derived from the free pay tax tables that are provided by the Inland Revenue or will be calculated by the payroll software based on the tax code given. This represents the total free pay to date. (Free pay is the equivalent of an annual tax allowance.)

Column 4b

This is for 'K' coded employees only (ie: those people who are under special circumstances and are notified to the employer by the Inland Revenue) and represents additional pay also derived from the free pay tax tables.

Column 5

This is the total taxable pay to date derived by taking the total pay to date (column 3) less free pay or plus additional pay (using either column 4a or 4b accordingly).

Column 6

This represents the total tax due to date and is obtained from the tax tables.

Columns 6a and 6b

This is for 'K' coded employees only and special rates apply.

Column 7

This represents the amount deducted or refunded for the given period. Refunds are denoted with the letter 'R'.

Column 8

This is applicable to 'K' codes only.

The above is the minimum information required for Form P11 (1996), but the Practice may wish to produce more detailed information either on the same sheet or appended to additional reports. Such information might include the net pay or the split between the Practice contribution (30%) and that reimbursed (70%) or, for PMS Contract Practices, those staff paid from within the overall sum and not from the staff allocation.

Whatever additional information you choose to keep with your records, the minimum requirements must be met. Remember that the employee's NI contributions and tax due will be taken from their gross salary, but the employer's contribution is an additional cost on top of the gross salary. As a guide, when the Practice is considering making a new appointment, it is advisable to calculate the expense to the Practice as being the gross salary plus a 13.0% of the gross salary. Using this calculation should ensure that all the employment costs have been anticipated.

The Month End

At the end of each tax month, which officially is the 5th day of the following month, the Practice is liable to pay any tax and NI due to the Collector of Taxes within 14 days and no later than the 19th of the given month. The amount paid to the Collector will represent all monies owed in respect of income tax and National Insurance contributions based on the tax deducted from employees (adjusted for any refunds due) and including both employees' and employers' NI contributions. Normally, as an existing employer you will be sent the appropriate payment book from the Inland Revenue. A cheque or transfer is normally arranged in favour of the Collector of Taxes. The Collector of Taxes (who is empowered to collect tax that is due) should not be confused with the Inspector of Taxes (who is responsible for the process of determining the tax that is due). Very often the two are based in different offices. All tax and NIC is paid together under the PAYE system and does not have to be accounted for separately to the DSS and the Inland Revenue.

If the required level of tax and NIC is not paid to the Collector of Taxes by the 19th following the month concerned, a reminder letter will normally be issued by the following 5th of the month. If the payment is still not received a final reminder will be received within two weeks of the first reminder, stating that the amount is still due and that if it is not paid, that the Practice is likely to be inspected. Therefore whilst it is possible for a return to be made late, the Inland Revenue frown upon persistent cases and will instigate inspection proceedings. An instigated inspection rather than a random review will almost certainly be more stringent.

The Year End

At the end of each tax year (ie: 5th April) and the following 19th of April, the Practice must submit a return (Form P14) to the Inspector of Taxes which details (for each member of staff employed during the tax year):

- The total pay received

- The total tax paid

- The total NI paid

- The employee's NI number and contribution rate and

- The taxable earnings (including Statutory Sick Pay and Statutory Maternity Pay).

The P14 return can be quite a long job to complete, so it is advisable to commence the process well before the19th April. At the same time, the Practice must complete additional forms. The P35 Form is a summary of all the P14s and must be sent with a covering statutory certificate (issued by the Inland Revenue). The other forms that must completed at this time are the employees' individual P60s, which detail the personal information contained within the P14 and must be supplied to each individual employee. As of April 1997, Form P60 must be given or sent to all employees by no later than 31st May of the year concerned.

Tax Codes

The employees' tax codes could be amended at any time throughout the tax year and it is vitally important that any new tax codes are implemented at the correct time. The tax code is the means by which an individual is assessed on his or her personal circumstances and when this code is used in conjunction with the tax tables (see below), it is possible to work out the exact taxation liability for each employee. As an employer, it is not your responsibility to agree the tax code with the Inland Revenue. That responsibility lies with the employee. Therefore, if an employee questions that the wrong code is being used, you must ask the employee to produce an Amended Code Form (P9)T in order that the new code can be used. You should not adjust an employee's code without the proper authority from the Inland Revenue.

The Tax Tables

The tax tables are a collection of figures provided by the Revenue that facilitate the calculation of the amount of tax due by an individual. There are actually three types of tax tables:

- Free Pay: Table A
- Taxable Pay: Tables B,C and D
- Tax Reckoner: Table F

Payroll Tip

Payroll is a complex subject and therefore errors can occur. However, if the Practice regularly reviews the work of the person completing the payroll, problems can often be avoided or anticipated before there is any financial embarrassment that affects the Practice. One phone call to the local DSS or Tax office can often answer any query you might have. Alternatively take advice from your accountant. Remember that the Inland Revenue and DSS will help you and also provide many free publications and leaflets. This is a free resource, so make sure you use it.

Staff Pensions

This is an issue that has been in the limelight for many years and attitudes to this matter vary from one practice to another. Staff should have been given the option whether or not to join the NHS pension scheme. The benefits for a practice belonging to such a scheme include:

- Maintaining good staff/employer relations

- An attractive employment benefit to offer when recruiting

- Creating greater staff loyalty

- Potential tax relief on contributions.

Careful consideration should be given to the operation of a staff pension scheme, but many proactive practices already reward key staff in this way. At least one person in the Practice should be aware about the operation of the NHS scheme or pension advice expertise should be made available to the Practice. Where doctors' spouses appear on the payroll, it can be a very efficient way to save for future retirement. Providing that the Practice can demonstrate that the spouse provides a service to the Practice, the salary can be pensionable therefore contributing to the joint savings of the GP. Indeed, there are cases where the Revenue allows the spouse to undertake a minimum amount of work in the surgery and is then allowed to be remunerated by virtue of the Practice paying the appropriate pension contributions.

CHAPTER 6

INCOME GENERATION

GP Status and Remuneration Levels

Introduction

Across the nation, there is a wide variation in the earnings of registered GPs – with some GPs receiving annual earnings that are thousands of pounds greater than others. There are reasons for these wide variations. Sometimes it is due to the type of reimbursements the Practice can attract; sometimes it is down to local policy; but very often it is due to prudence and good housekeeping which minimises cost and maximises profit.

The GP Contract with the NHS provides for the potential of earning a predictable sum for a given number of hours. Additional hours can be worked to increase income, but analysis of profits has shown there is a limit at which NHS or GMS work remains profitable and greater profit can be achieved by supplementing income through private and other associated work. The introduction of the PMS Contract effectively allowed an opportunity to negotiate an agreed Contract Sum, which could be compared to an annual salary. One key fact is becoming evident: more and more of GPs' remuneration will be determined by capitation-based ratios and formulae. As we have already discussed, this principle is also the basis of the new GMS Contract where a financial value is ascribed to each patient.

Prudent practices have already established protocols for screening new patients and therefore predicting their potential net worth to the Practice. Therefore a stable or growing list size is an important indicator in the financial health of the Practice.

GP Status

The introduction of the GP Contract during 1990 earmarked a clear definition of the contractor status. Over a decade later, we are looking at the introduction of yet another type of GMS Contract. The GP is an independently self-employed individual who holds a contract with the NHS and is free to earn income elsewhere. The General Practitioner is therefore classed as self-employed or as a sole trader or partnership and taxation matters are dealt with under Schedule D.

Whilst the role of the GP continues without too much question from the Inland Revenue, the nature of any potential partnerships (with or without Partnership Agreements) means that General Practice is subject to more intensive review by the Revenue – particularly when there are trainees, salaried doctors or clinical assistants employed.

It is the definition of "control" which separates employer from employee. The General Practitioner works in an environment of self-regulation and control. He or she is self-employed or is employed by the Practice – but is not an employee of the PCT. The introduction of a new, locally managed GMS Contract heralds a window of opportunity to operate General Practice in a much more flexible way while still retaining the potential to earn a good living.

The Practice

It would be fair to say that no two practices are ever run in exactly the same way. It is true that no two businesses would be run exactly the same either, unless maybe there was some form of franchise operation being run. However, the nature of General Practice is not that of a franchise, although some Trusts might wish them to be run that way. By allowing the Practice to innovate and develop itself, it helps the Practice to provide a greater range of services, which in turn will shape the overall profitability of the Practice. Conversely many will see this ability for diversification as being a threat to overall patient needs in the belief that, by offering more services, GPs will not be concentrating on the traditional, core primary care services. It is for these sorts of reasons that there is so often debate or confrontation about how services should be developed.

The language of business is finance and the system should be flexible enough to allow enterprise and initiative to flow. Finance is the key factor in business operations. In business, flexible financial arrangements have been shown to encourage enterprise and new initiatives. A similar principle should apply to General Practice. The introduction of GP Fundholding allowed additional services to be developed and offered within the Practice, but only over the last couple of years have we seen the relaxing of rules in order that GPs can be remunerated for additional secondary care work that they undertake for commissioners (such as the NHS and PCTs).

The government change in May 1997 heralded the dawn of another period of transition. Fundholding was no longer the preferred option, but the new government seemed keen to adopt the best parts of all models, including Fundholding. This has opened the door for opportunities for individuals and groups of practices to be more innovative about the services they offer. With the NHS moving towards being Primary Care-led, it is imperative that the people given the task to make it happen (ie: the GPs) are rewarded for their efforts.

Under Fundholding the GP has complete managerial control. Under the new GP Contracts the GP has gained more ways in which to attract reimbursement but has lost complete overall control.

Some people regard such changes as moves towards privatisation – with General Practice increasingly being put into private management and using commercial principles. Whether or not you view the GP Contracts as moves towards privatisation – in an ethical or philosophical sense if not technically speaking – it is true to say that the running of a modern General Practice is now governed by many rules and regulations.

All political issues put aside, everyone who works for a living is looking to achieve the best possible pay for the least hours to achieve the maximum independence. It is only when you have comfortably achieved your personal financial goals that you can consider other options in the secure knowledge that your future is protected.

The question of privatisation should not even be an issue for the GP. However, the question of profit is an issue – and one that should be addressed regularly. Only if General Practice became salaried would profit cease to be an issue as it would then be replaced by incentive schemes and/or performance-related pay.

How is GP Income Decided?

How much should a GP be paid? Each individual GP will have their own answer to this question, but it is accepted that any negotiations about increases to fees and allowances is done in conjunction with the Doctors' Pay Review Body. Following a government review and recommendations, the Body was set up in 1960 with the task of reporting to the government about future pay and remuneration levels. The Review Body considered many options but revolves around certain key principles:

- The Review Body will exercise best judgement to all decisions

- The Review Body judgements are accepted by the government (although government does have the power of veto)

- Decisions made by the Review Body are enacted promptly

- Remuneration levels are determined by comparison with other like professionals

- Doctors' remuneration should not be used as a vehicle by the government to influence other economic decisions

- All decisions should reflect a long-term view and not be valued according to short-term peaks and troughs of demand.

The Review Body looks at evidence obtained from the medical profession (normally provided by the British Medical Association) and at the same time considers written evidence from Health Departments. A lot of the information considered will be based on written evidence obtained throughout the year and concluded by negotiation. Actual statistical data are then collected and GPs salaries are compared. This information will then be complemented by the Review Body's own independent evidence and once both sides have exchanged information the process is concluded by means of oral hearings and meetings. The final stage is a confidential appraisal submitted to the Prime Minister together with a list of recommendations. The final decision is announced by the Prime Minister some time later.

Having looked at the mechanism by which overall GP pay is decided, we now need to examine the way in which fee income actually reaches the GP.

The NHS, by means of the GP Contract, agrees to pay contractors gross income out of which certain practice expenses must be paid. This gross income is therefore designed to both cover costs and provide a certain level of income or profit. Therefore, combine the recommended level of net income for GPs and the method of review and we start to see how the Annual Statement of Fees and Allowances are computed. Herein lies the first key problem. Although the final decision of the government will determine the average earnings of a general practitioner, there are a number of key factors that will mean that no two practices will share an average profit potential and there will be widespread national variation.

Having established the means by which a net profit can be achieved, it is important that the next element be taken into consideration. This is the reimbursement of certain expenses that can be claimed in full and therefore income matches expenditure. Some of these reimbursements will be paid direct to the Practice, but some may be directly reimbursable to an individual GP. Therefore, within each practice there must be an incentive for the Practice to consider cost efficiencies overall and for individual GPs to consider how to maximise economies for individuals' expenses.

GP Financial and Parity Status

Before it is possible to determine an individual GP's guaranteed level of income, it is important to consider whether or not a Profit-Share applies. (Profit-Share agreements usually only apply to Partnerships but some single-handed GPs may also have Profit-Share agreements with non-clinical staff.)

With more and more GPs retiring and less and less entering the profession, the status of GPs and the profit earned by the GP varies widely.

There is currently a shortage of GPs entering General Practice and Partnerships. In previous years, it was accepted that an incoming partner would 'buy' into his or her share of the Practice to obtain full parity. However, nowadays there is a trend for some GPs to enter a practice and agree to do a certain amount of work for an agreed sum without having to buy into the Practice.

Very often incoming partners will avoid 'buying in' to own their own share of the Practice. In some cases this can be because they do not wish to buy a share of the Practice premises. Following the property boom of the 1980s, General Practice fell foul to the exorbitant price escalations, which now means, following subsequent rent reviews, many practices are faced with situations of negative equity – and, very naturally, incoming Partners can be reluctant to take on such a financial burden. This means that an outgoing partner may well want the Practice to be valued at the level at which or she purchased it but the incoming Partner almost certainly would not want to buy in to something which is actually worth less than the asking price.

This is just one example (albeit a very common one) of why partnerships are not always apportioned equally. Choices made by individuals can now mean that GP status within any one partnership vary widely and this serves to illustrate why there is a need for clear and unambiguous Partnership Agreements. Without such Agreements, there can be disputes about the financial status of the GPs within the Partnership. Indeed, there is still a considerable amount of variation in the terms and conditions under which Partnership Agreements are formulated.

Remuneration Levels

There are three main levels of remuneration, which contribute to the overall income of an individual GP:

- Effort-related income (eg: where work is carried out and paid for such as maternity or immediately necessary treatments)

- Fixed income (eg: these are payments irrespective of the actual amount of work done, such as the basic practice allowance)

- Private income (eg: this could be for providing a secondary service such as colposcopy or private medical reports).

Under a PMS Contract, these items are still considered when setting the baseline funding (the minimum guaranteed sum for the Practice). It is likely the new GMS Contract will also refer to historic performance when calculating remuneration levels.

The structure of a GP's income is dependent on various factors, for example:

- Whether or not the minimum level of contract work has been achieved (or even exceeded)

- Over-achieving of targets – which could help a practice to eventually move to a higher level under the GMS Contract but would not necessarily attract additional funding in the short-term

- Cases where a GP concentrates on his or her private patients (and private income) while neglecting their NHS patients, employing locums and, thus, alienating patients who may transfer to other practices.

To achieve maximum profitability the practice should strive to:

- Ensure that the minimum requirements under the terms of the GP contract have been achieved

- Check frequently the patient list to make sure that the Practice has identified all the patients for whom the Practice is entitled to claim allowances - and to make sure that those allowances are processed accordingly

- Resolve issues about any 'disputed' patients with the Primary Care Trust as soon as possible

- Review any 'effort-related' income to ensure that the best return is being achieved from an individual's time

- Maximise private income while still giving consideration to the time and effort put in by the individual GP.

The key to achieving the maximum level of remuneration is to have a realistic understand of the true return on the amount of effort and expense invested. This is otherwise known as the profit margin. The larger the profit margin, the larger the sums that can be retained by the Practice and the individual GP.

For example, it may be more profitable for a partnership to agree to allow one partner to earn private income by providing a service while the other GPs in the Practice to cover his or her practice sessions with the agreement that everyone gets a fair share of the overall profit. Without everyone's agreement and support, it wouldn't be possible for the individual partner to earn that extra private income which will benefit all the GPs in the Practice. Such arrangements are to be encouraged as a profitable approach to running the GP Practice.If all partners try and do a bit of everything (without such an arrangement), it is likely that only marginal profit is going to be realised.

So it would seem that there is a clear structure to the overall Practice remuneration levels. It is important that the GPs within an individual practice gain a good understanding of this structure and its implications for the control and flexibility of Practice finances – and, consequently, the profitability of the Practice and the remuneration for the individual members of the Practice.

Other Income

There are numerous fees and allowances that a practice can claim, but even claiming all of these will not necessarily be the most profitable way of maximising profit. Providing the Practice is fulfilling its obligations under the terms of service of the GP Contract, it is free (by virtue of its self-employed status) to look at alternative means of income generation.

The types of alternative income can be very varied and fluctuate from a one-off fee payment to a three-year contract for services. The only catch is that the local Primary Care Trust can make a deduction against certain direct expenses if the private income of the Practice exceeds 10% of the total gross practice income.

Again this illustrates the importance of adopting a balanced approach and emphasises the need for careful analysis of all Practice income. It is generally accepted that a practice that concentrates purely on NHS work and services covered by the GMS Contract will only ever attract average remuneration packages for its GPs. Most practices, whose profit per partner ratio is significantly higher than average earnings, utilise a combination of income opportunities derived from the private sector.

One factor that is quite critical to this process is that more and more people have (or are being provided with) private medical insurance cover and as a result it is possible for GP practices to undertake a number of private insurance or medical reports each year. If the Practice can become assigned to a particular insurance company for insurance medical reports, this can be an almost guaranteed source of referral for the Practice. As with the private sector, public sector medicals can also be an attractive source of income, especially if the Practice is asked to tender to provide a public health role to a local council or authority. This kind of income will be received over a given period and therefore gives the Practice the reassurance and security of known source of income during that period.

Every patient on the Practice list is a potential source of income for the Practice – whether it be the long-distance lorry driver who needs to renew his driving license or someone going on holiday wanting inoculations or simply passport applications. Each of these procedures often take little time and attract a fixed fee normally based on suggested rates published by the British Medical Association.

School medicals, occupational health schemes for local businesses, services to residential care homes and to public service bodies (such as the local police or prison service) are just a few examples of how a practitioner can earn additional income. Relaxation in local rules means that out-of-hours cover and locum cover can also provide potential income.

In addition, Primary Care Trusts, who now have direct control of the commissioning of GP services, are looking more and more to the primary care setting to provide secondary care services. Typical examples of these types of secondary services include: minor surgery, colposcopy and diabetic clinics. The list for new secondary services is growing, particularly as GPs can now shift some of the clinical management of their list to practice nurses and even more to nurse practitioners.

As already discussed earlier, many GPs now provide session work for Hospital Trusts. It will be easier with local working arrangements and purpose-built premises to transfer these services into primary care settings. Opportunities will arise for like-minded practices to pool resources to work together and this can also involve single-handed GPs who may choose to provide such services to Hospital Trusts or to larger GP practices.

The key to maximising income levels under the PMS Contract and the new GMS Contract is negotiation with the PCT primarily and other GP practices as appropriate. With good negotiation, the Practice will be able to set the Contract value at a level that, in theory, will allow a pre-determined level of superannuated pay. Secondly, by continuously monitoring the performance of the Practice against the agreed contract performance levels, the Practice will be better able to ensure that additional workloads are not undertaken for which no reimbursement is received. Applying for contract variations (such as a significant change in list size) or exceptional circumstances (such as a temporary increase in the local population) can overcome the problem of not claiming all the due reimbursement, but past performance has shown that this is not always readily reciprocated by the PCT.

Lastly, controlling expenditure will not actually generate more income, but, with good management, it will help to ensure that your profit is greater.

CHAPTER 7

EXPENDITURE AND RESOURCE ALLOCATIONS

Personal Expenses and Making the Most of Capital Allowances

Introduction

The very first thing to be aware of about the claiming of personal expenses or business expenses paid privately is that the Inland Revenue Inspector is well within his or her rights to challenge any claim made. For an item to qualify for tax relief, it must satisfy the Wholly and Exclusively Rule by being only used for business purposes. There are times when an item may have both personal and business uses and the Revenue may well challenge claims for such items. For example, a land line telephone in a GP surgery would almost certainly satisfy the Wholly and Exclusively Rule whereas a claim for a GP's mobile telephone may be more questionable (as the mobile telephone is probably used for business and personal calls.)

Who Pays?

Deciding who is responsible for which items and documenting this policy may well lead to the avoidance of costly mistakes or potentially damaging areas of contention between partners. Care must be taken because so many people can be involved: partners may not always agree with each other, the accountant may not always agree with the partners and the Inspector of Taxes may disagree with both the accountant and the partners – and so it carries on. The typical areas that cause disputes include:

- Home expenses
- Motor and travel expenses
- Subscriptions

- Locum fees

- Private fees

- Spouses salary

- Telephone bills

- Equipment costs.

Of these, perhaps the areas of spouses' salaries and motoring expenses cause the majority of disagreements.

The list above provides examples but there are other areas that cause dispute. The Practice should look at ways of defining what is and what is not acceptable as legitimate Practice expense. By doing this as part of (or as an addendum to) the Practice Partnership Agreement (or Deed), will ensure that the Practice follows a consistent approach and disputes with all parties are avoided. Remember that costs will be incurred if precious time is spent sorting out disputes at partnership level, when such disputes could have been avoided simply by adopting a policy throughout the Practice.

All Schedule D taxpayers are subject to certain rules and guidelines – including the 'Wholly and Exclusively Rule discussed above. To avoid problems with the Inspector of Taxes, the Practice should adopt a policy early on which details all types of expenses and whether they do or do not meet the 'Wholly and Exclusively' criteria. Partners should all complete and verify (with their signature) a return detailing their expenses that meet the 'Wholly and Exclusively' criteria. This return should coincide with the year end accounting date even if the partner only joined the Practice mid-year. Where there is a claim for an expense that is for part-private and part-business use, it is advisable to let your accountant negotiate a tax relief claim with the Inspector of Taxes on your behalf. There is a need for a fine balance given that wherever there is 'Duality of Purpose' the Inland Revenue is within their rights to disallow all or part of the expenditure under question. Whilst it is rare for items such as motoring expenses to be disallowed, there are many instances where the doctor seeks to obtain tax relief on a number of items only to find them being disallowed completely.

It has become a well-known fact that, with the introduction of the Taxpayers' Charter, the Inland Revenue uses a number of techniques to identify false claims. Sometimes individuals volunteer the information themselves but, when a false claim is suspected, the Inland Revenue will undertake a formal investigation. This means those areas such a motoring expenses, spouses' salary, use of home and telephone costs are particularly susceptible to further investigation. The Inland Revenue has the right to look into the previous six years of the tax affairs of the Practice and, if it emerges that the Practice has been incorrectly claiming some expenses, the Practice may have to pay backdated tax – and this could be quite costly.

Therefore, claims of this nature should be supported with as much documentation as possible and, wherever practical, estimates should be avoided. To have claims disallowed retrospectively, if proven to be a case of over-claiming, would not only cost the Practice a potentially large amount in terms of tax that was due but could also make the Practice liable for penalties and interest payments.

The best way to avoid all this trouble and expense is to ensure that all claims are submitted in a properly authorised claim form. In the event that questions are asked by the Inspector of Taxes, it will be possible to respond immediately with the necessary information. This, in a majority of cases, will be sufficient to satisfy the Inland Revenue and the investigation will cease. However, if this information is not immediately available, not only will the suspicions of the Revenue be aroused, but also it is likely to cost the Practice additional expense in accountancy fees to deal with the matter. Even then there will be no guarantee that the matter will be resolved in the favour of the Practice.

The Claim

It is not always easy to determine what items and expenses the Inland Revenue will allow you claim for tax relief. The Revenue do have the final say on what they will and will not accept. However, in general terms, the following categories of claims are usually accepted by the Inland Revenue:

- Expenses paid privately by the GP and can be clearly justified as Practice expenses
- Expenses paid privately by the GP which include a private element of use
- Estimated expenses

At the end of the day it is the doctors who are responsible for the information that is provided to prepare the accounts that are submitted to the Inland Revenue. It is no good thinking that if the Inland Revenue decide not to allow certain expenses it will be a matter that the accountant can resolve. Ultimately, it will still be the responsibility of the doctors in the Practice. The Inland Revenue undertakes random reviews and, therefore, if the information provided by a Practice is consistent, the Practice is less likely to be chosen for investigation. Forward thinking, coupled with consistency and reasonableness, will ensure that in the majority of cases there will be no further questions.

Due to the nature of General Practice, it is not uncommon that each Partner may employ their own accountant for their own individual tax purposes while another firm of accountants acts for the Partnership as a whole and prepares the Practice accounts. There is nothing wrong with this approach, other than there are more people with whom to liaise and the action of one party may accidentally overlap the action of another. If this type of arrangement does exist in the Practice, it is vitally important that each knows of the others' involvement in order that there is no duplication of effort, which could be costly to the doctors. Of course, it must not be forgotten that legally there is no reason why the Practice should not deal with its own affairs and liaise directly with the Revenue. The only point to mention is that the Practice may not have the specialist skills to negotiate effectively with the Revenue and as a rule, the Inspector of Taxes prefer to deal through an agent (usually an accountant) with whom they can be very direct at times.

Claiming for the Use of Your Home

At some time a GP will almost certainly use his or her own home for business purposes. This is particularly true of small single-handed practices who actually operate from their own home. Use of the home represents a legitimate claim for tax purposes. However, conversely there are those GPs who clearly operate from one or more surgeries and also live well away from their practice population area, but who may still use their own home for research or educational purposes. Before a claim for home use is submitted, the following criteria should be met:

- There must be clear proof that the house is used for the consulting or treating of patients on a regular basis

- A nameplate is displayed confirming the fact that a doctor practices from the premises (this is not mandatory, but definitely will act as further evidence if required)

- The house is situated within or close to the practice population it serves

- The doctor's name, address and telephone number is included in the local telephone directory

- Practice correspondence includes this address - again, this is not mandatory, but will assist with any claim

In any case, for a claim to be even considered, it must include clear evidence of genuine use. Assuming that the above can be established, the mechanism to determine the costs will need to be evaluated and documented. The Inland Revenue normally prefers to operate the overall costs associated with a points system, which relates to the overall size of the property, but other methods can be employed. Whatever method is used, it is important that the amount claimed represents the normal running costs adjusted for capital expenditure. The amount claimed only becomes justifiable if the Practice and home are one and the same building. In the event that from time-to-time the GPs may occasionally work from home, it is possible to look at claiming a form of study allowance. At the end of the day this amount could be questioned and any claim must be related to overall costs and represent a reasonable amount. It would not be sensible to put in a claim that represented say 50 hours per week. Any claim should also be reasonably adjusted to reflect holidays, ie: a 52 week year should be adjusted to say 46 weeks, allowing six weeks for holidays.

Having established a mechanism for recording expenses to be claimed, consideration should be given to some of the typical claim items. Each item in the following list may or may not be allowable subject to the individual Tax Inspector who is dealing with the claim. However, if the claim is properly prepared any of the following may be acceptable:

Use of own home items:	Potential claim:
Private bank charges	Part of charges
Private telephone costs	Part of charges
Security costs	Part of charges
Courses/conferences	Doctors expenses only (not spouses')
Front garden and access maintenance	Can be considered if claim made for genuine home use

Use of own home items:	Potential claim:
Insurance	Claim as part of home expenses
Personal accountancy fees	In full
Magazines and papers	Claim through Practice preferably
Cleaning and laundry	Except normal wear and tear
Medical equipment	In full
Books and journals	Claim through Practice preferably
Subscriptions	In full
Locum costs and fees	In full
Photography - cameras, film	Part of charges
Charitable donations	In full, subject to Revenue agreement
Computer equipment	Part of charges

The above list is only illustrative and may not be exhaustive, but gives a good indication of the types of expenses a general practitioner may be claiming. Wherever there is some form of reimbursement received by the practice, the claim will be disallowed on the basis that the cost has been repaid in full. These types of incidental costs could easily run into thousands of pounds of potentially tax deductible expenditure. Adopting a good policy of recording these types of transactions as and when they occur will mean it will be easier to defend any claim that is challenged. Potentially, tax liabilities can be drastically reduced by paying detailed attention to often-neglected areas of expense.

Motoring and Travel Expenses

Motoring and travel expenses are dealt with as a separate matter due to the complexity and the number of different items that this category includes. There is normally no problem in agreeing part-use of a private vehicle for Practice purposes. The final amount agreed will depend upon the outcome of negotiations with the Inland Revenue. Normally, the value of the vehicle will have been agreed amongst the partners and each will have a car of similar value. However, this is not always the case and this can sometimes cause friction between partners. In general, all motoring and travel costs should be supported by the appropriate receipts/invoices and, as ever, estimates should only be used in extreme cases. As a minimum the costs submitted should include the following:

- Interest on loan finance (this may be restricted)
- Hire purchase interest
- Road tax
- Insurance premiums (including cover for business use)
- Petrol/diesel
- Maintenance
- Servicing
- Oil
- MOT certificate costs
- Car parking charges
- Car washing /valeting charges

Doctors may also claim for travel by public transport and taxi as long as receipts or invoices can be produced as proof of the expenditure. Travel by public transport or taxi is normally 100% allowable but travel by car will usually be allowed subject to an adjustment for private use.

Remember that, a claim which is made will need to justifiable and the best way of doing this is to provide an analysis of mileage over say a three-month period. This is not to say that a claim may go through unchallenged, but if a mileage review is made periodically, it will mean that the doctor is in a better position to defend his claim, if questioned. Keeping such records may also help the doctor to identify when his or her mileage has in fact increased and this could lead to them being able to increase their claim with the Inland Revenue.

Some doctors may wish to claim for more than one car and this in itself may not be unreasonable. However, the amount claimed is the determining factor and to claim say 80% on both cars may prove unrealistic, but say 90% on one car and 25% on the other may be seen as more reasonable. Where two cars are involved, a detailed log of information and mileage is definitely preferable, due to the fact that such an arrangement will almost certainly undergo periodic review by the Inland Revenue. The value of the vehicle is restricted as far as capital allowances are concerned, so it is better to reach agreement on the value of the car to avoid arguments later. Capital allowances will be given subject to the overall restriction each year at a rate of 25% of the residual value of the car. Therefore, if there is a reason or policy for changing cars, it would be sensible to do it towards the end of the Practice financial year. By doing this, the allowances on the new vehicle qualify on the preceding year basis and therefore attracts to the Practice the maximum use of allowances a year earlier. This means that it is possible for the GP to offset the tax advantages on a new vehicle almost one year earlier than if the vehicle had been purchased at the beginning of the financial year – and this can represent a considerable saving.

Given that so much expenditure is reimbursed or grant monies are paid to general practitioners it can be very misleading regarding the treatment of items for capital allowances. Be warned the Inland Revenue is not likely to entertain the practice of attempting to claim double relief, ie: by claiming reimbursement in full and also annual capital allowances. However, there may be a number of items to which relief can be claimed correctly. For example, if a practice buys computer equipment it can attract a capital allowance. However, if they are reimbursed fully for this item, then no allowance can be claimed. If they are partly reimbursed, then they can make a partial claim.

Spouses' Salaries, Pensions and Retirement

These elements have been linked together due to the relationship, in more than one sense of the word, that each of these items has with each other. Effective planning throughout the lifetime of general practice will guarantee retirement at a chosen date on chosen terms. Choosing to ignore the potential gains at the early stages will result in the sad situation of not being able to retire at a chosen date and certainly not on the anticipated or expected terms. Doctors have often thought that their unique position of qualifying for the NHS superannuation scheme was sufficient security for a planned and perfect retirement, but as with many long-term investments of this nature, nothing is guaranteed and therefore returns must be constantly reviewed and supplemented if necessary.

If the GP has a spouse who is earning less than the 40% tax threshold, then the GP can consider paying the spouse a notional salary to allow pension contributions to be made and also to obtain relief from taxation. In effect, the couple would be pooling their taxable income. Such a salary might not attract reimbursement from the PCT, but it can help to reduce taxation.

CHAPTER 8

YOUR ACCOUNTANT AND UNDERSTANDING YOUR ACCOUNTS

Introduction

The purpose of this chapter is to demonstrate how to get the best working relationship with your accountant and minimise the costs of employing professional advice. There is no question that you pay for quality of work and a high fee should reflect an equally high quality service. However, very often, general practitioners fall into the trap of misusing the services of their accountant and obviously feel frustrated at often having to pay high fees. With a bit of forethought and early planning a lot of unnecessary accountancy fees can be avoided and you will use the professional expertise you purchase to maximise profitability within the Practice.

How to Reduce Your Accountancy Fees

Your accountant is running a business too! He or she is always looking for more work because the more work they have the more fees they can charge. It may be advisable to use an accountant but it is not a statutory requirement. However, when you use an accountant you can reduce you accountancy fees by undertaking some tasks in the Practice rather than asking the accountant to do them. By giving your accountant more work to do you will make him or her very happy because you will be paying higher fees. However, it is possible to reduce the amount of work you accountant undertakes on your behalf without actually making a great deal of extra effort within the Practice. The following is a simple illustration of how to make your accountant very happy (and how to find yourself facing unnecessarily high accountancy fees!)

Dr Profitt is not the best organised of doctors but insists on dealing personally with all the financial matters of the Practice - much to the annoyance of the other two partners. However, Dr Profitt is the Senior Partner and the other partners know that he will retire in the next few years. Dr Profitt uses the services of Bloggs and Co, a city accountancy firm. Bloggs and Co are a commercially orientated firm with no real expertise in General Practice accounts, but the senior accountant has been known to Dr Profitt for many years. Dr Profitt and his partners have commented on the fees charged for the past couple of years but have been advised that the escalating fees relate mainly to the following items:

THE ITEMS	ACCOUNTANTS' DELIGHT (extra fees to charge!) - £££
No completed cash book is kept	Incomplete records
Cash book is not totalled	Junior Clerk task
Illegible documentation	Write to Client
Inadequate Information	Write to Client
No detailed list of expenses paid privately	Write and Meet with Client
Bank Statements not complete	Incomplete Records
Petty Cash not reconciled	Incomplete Records
Not answering letters	Reminders!
Send wrong information	Second Request!
Request amendments to the accounts	Whoopee, extra fee!
Submit the accounts late	It's appeal time again!
Omit to complete tax return	Are they serious?
Inland Revenue investigation	Could be time to retire!

The above is a just a jovial portrayal of the types of events that will put a smile on the accountant's face and add weight to his wallet. In general, many practices fail to have the controls in place which would dramatically reduce the time and cost of employing the services of qualified professionals. To this end many accountants are used incorrectly and instead of providing services to compliment the Practice and enhance profitability, many accountants are used for no more than a glorified bookkeeping service.

The nature of General Practice is such that at the very least the doctors should be convinced that whoever represents their practice has certain rudimentary skills as far as the NHS and General Practice is concerned. An understanding of the Statement of Fees and Allowances is important, as well as those factors that affect General Practice directly, such as GP Fundholding or Locality-Based Commissioning. Very often the accountancy approach adopted for General Practice is significantly different from that used in dealing with commercial organisations – and specialist accountancy skills may be required.

The accountant will produce accounts for the Practice, which detail the financial performance of the Practice and also demonstrate the net worth of the Partners. Doctors should insist on accounts being written in a format that they can readily understand. Very often accounts are presented in the fashion chosen by the accountant, but the doctors (as owners of the accounts) should influence the way the information is presented. Unlike limited companies, which must account in a prescribed manner, the average sole practitioner or partnership is free to present the accounts in the format that most benefits their own understanding. Sometimes the accounts will be drawn up in a summarised format for use in the Practice and for forwarding to the Inland Revenue, with more detailed management accounts provided for more detailed analysis. Whatever the format adopted, the doctors must understand the information presented to them, because the process of signing the accounts is equivalent to accepting full legal responsibility for what is contained in the accounts, even though the doctors may not have actually prepared the information themselves.

What Are Accounts Used For?

The accounts and the way they are prepared can be used for a number of different purposes. These are outlined below:

Purpose of Accounts	How They Are Used
Tax liabilities	Inland Revenue agreement
Financing loans	Lender will evaluate risk
Management Information	Current and Future performance of the Practice
Fee Income	To show value of various sources of fee income and compare worth to practice
Efficiency	To review expenditure and plan costs against budgets to achieve additional profit
The Retiring Partner	To evaluate net worth on retirement
The New Partner	To evaluate potential future earnings

Purpose of Accounts	How They Are Used
The Partnership Agreement/Deed	Normally a deed will stipulate the requirement that accounts are prepared and made available to all partners
Payments Review Body	Each year a sampling process is undertaken on random GP accounts which help shape the value of future levels of reimbursement
Personal Borrowing..................................	House mortgage requirement

The following is an illustration of what a set of accounts might contain for an average GP Practice. The detail shown is not exhaustive and may vary more or less (subject to the requirements of the individual practice).

Firstly the accounts contain a statement to certify the accounts. The statement is made by the accountant(s) who have prepared the accounts and is often worded:

'We have prepared the following income and expenditure statement on pages 1 -2, together with the attached balance sheet and notes from the vouchers and records produced to us and from the explanations given to us. We have not carried out an audit.'

Understanding this statement is important. By virtue that it is included in your annual accounts does not mean that the accounts may be free from error or that the accountants accept any responsibility. This certificate must not be confused with a 'reporting accountants' or 'registered auditors' certificate which actually confirms an opinion and establishes a true and fair view. This certificate simply verifies that the work has been carried out professionally, but gives no more assurances than that. Indeed, such a certificate will not mean that the Inland Revenue will not investigate the detail of the accounts. It is vital that if there is anything that causes concern, that these matters are discussed with the accountants before the 'draft' accounts are finalised and signed. Remember that, once the accounts have been signed they become the responsibility of the taxpayer. However, in the event that genuine errors are discovered it is possible, in many cases, that adjustments can be made in future years or in extreme cases the accounts can be re-opened and agreement with the Tax Inspector settled locally.

The Profit and Loss Account and the Balance Sheet

There are two key tools used in preparing your accounts. These are:

- The Profit and Loss Account (also know as the Income and Expenditure Statement), and

- The Balance Sheet

In a General Practice, the Profit and Loss Account shows a break down of income from NHS and private sources. It also defines those items that have been reimbursed. There is a comparison made with the previous year's performance, which makes it easy to see any major shifts in income or expenditure. Expenditure is broken down into key components. Again this makes analysis easier and also it makes it more suitable for analysing those costs that could be influenced by the practice directly. Where further explanation in desirable, reference is made to the notes contained with the accounts that provide the detail. This is often necessary due to the fact that not all income is recognised as being Practice income and may be attributed to individual partners. This effect can distort how the profit share is perceived.

The Balance Sheet is used to calculate the actual financial position of the Practice year-on-year and takes into account money owed by the Practice, money held by the Practice and money due to the Practice.

An example of a typical Profit and Loss Account is given overleaf. It is followed by an example of the corresponding Balance Sheet. Naturally, the figures included in the illustration are examples only and should not be deemed as being illustrative of any actual practice.

Dr Profitt
Profit and Loss Account for the Year Ended 31 March 2003

	2003 (£)	2002 (£)
INCOME		
National Health Service		
Capitation Fees	26,948	23,476
Items of Service	3,500	3,438
Maternity	1,625	1,525
Practice Allowances	14,100	10,251
Reimbursements		
Rent and Rates	8,541	8,042
Ancillary Staff	13,526	11,252
National Insurance	1,300	1,200
Locum Fees	500	500
Total Income	70,040	59,684
EXPENDITURE		
Practice Expenses		
Locum Fees	3,526	1,525
Equipment Maintenance	65	50
Relief Services	850	750
Staff Expenses		
Ancillary Staff	12,099	12,035
National Insurance	1,300	1,200
Premises Expenses		
Rent	8,020	8,005
Rates	859	845
Heating and Lighting	580	568
Administration Expenses		
Printing and Stationery	425	504
Telephone	745	895
Bank Charges	36	48
Total Expenditure	28,505	26,425
Net Profit for the Year	41,535	33,259

Dr Profitt
Balance Sheet as at 31 March 2003

	2003 (£)	2002 (£)
Fixed Assets	4,500	4,500
Property	25,000	25,000
Current Assets		
Debtors	800	1,200
Cash at Bank	235	0
	1,035	1,200
Current Liabilities		
Bank Overdraft	0	2,300
Creditors	4,552	4,452
	4,552	6,752
Net Current Assets/(liabilities)	(3,517)	(5,552)
Total Assets less Current Liabilities	25,983	23,948
Financed by Capital Accounts		
Dr Profitt Current Account	(3,517)	(5,552)
Dr Profitt Capital Account	29,500	29,500
	25,983	23,948

Again (as with the Profit and Loss Account) there is very often, particularly in larger partnerships, a need for further explanatory notes required to accompany the Balance Sheet. These notes might describe the composition or movement of the Asset Accounts (such as fixtures and fittings or vehicles) and, especially, the actual amount of cash held in the Partners' Current and Capital Accounts. If no breakdown is made between the individual partners, then it will be difficult in the future, without preparing new accounts to differentiate between costs and income attributed to each. When drawing up the accounts, as much detail as possible should be included to allow full comprehension of the summarised accounts. This open approach between partners will avoid disputes, may also avoid the need (and expense) of having to re-open the accounts at a later date and could help to avoid the need for unnecessarily protracted dealings with the Inland Revenue.

Although it is not obligatory to provide notes to accompany the accounts, it is good practice to provide the owners of the accounts sufficient information to allow meaningful judgements to be made about the GP Practice and individual partners. Whilst a good set of accounts may look pleasing to a potential lender, (for example a bank or prospective mortgage lender) further detailed analysis of Partner Capital Accounts might reveal that the doctor concerned is better or worse off than the summarised accounts would leave the reader to believe. For example: the actual Practice accounts will demonstrate the overall financial stability of the Practice but the notes to accompany the accounts might show that one GP has a higher share within the Practice

The notes that accompany the accounts may consist of some or all of the following:

Accounting Policies – these are designed to bring to the reader's attention any treatment of income or expenditure within the accounts which is not in line with normal practice

List Size - given that so much nowadays relates to list size, it may be appropriate to record the numbers of patients on the Practice list during the period of the accounts. Such information will help year-to-year analysis and facilitate the notification of any obvious errors

Fixed Assets – these relate in particular to the Practice premises, although, if the Practice has more than one surgery, it is necessary to show all asset types separately

Capital Accounts - it is important that the Partner accounts are analysed in order that the correct level of tax liability can be apportioned. When comparing drawings levels they are adjusted against individual current accounts and reduced or increased accordingly

In some cases a further analysis of drawings is made to clearly identify who is being paid and when. Many practices do not review regularly the level of drawings, but it is good practice (and may help to avoid the expensive position of being overdrawn) if the drawings are reviewed regularly in line with the actual cashflow of the practice. If managed properly, this should help to avoid the complicated situation of doctors drawing more money out of the Practice that the amount of which they have paid tax.

Key Management Ratios

Introduction

The purpose of this section is to investigate the worth of using management ratios in General Practice and how quick interpretation of results can lead to efficiency and overall profitability. Management ratios are a simple effective method of analysing data to identify any significant variation to the consistent running of a practice.

Management ratios can be used to determine the progress on longer-term strategies, but also can be used to inform effective short-term decision making. Like business in general, the Practice environment is subject to almost constant change and each change can, and normally does, bring new opportunities and potential profits or losses to the overall practice.

Some larger practices may have diversified with a number of different income opportunities and the use of ratios will allow the Practice to evaluate and understand the contributions made by different areas of the Practice.

The common language of any business is financial and to that end it follows that the key ratios being explored are financially based. However, when such ratios are evaluated, the reality of the situation may mean more than just financial adjustments and may result in a complete adjustment of existing working practices. The ratios being reviewed are simply a quick way of measuring current performance and it is the day-to-day workings of the Practice that must be managed and not simply the ratios.

The statistics derived from the management rations can tell us certain things – but they are not an end in themselves. Good management uses statistics but relies on proper analysis and an understanding of how and why circumstances can change in order to maintain control of the business.

The Use of Good Data

Even if the financial information being presented is good, very often it is presented in a format that is difficult to comprehend or leaves the reader bemused and therefore disinterested with the issues being presented. Therefore it is the intention of this section to concentrate only on specific areas that will be of direct use to the busy General Practice. The key issues affecting the Practice finances will be:

- The assets of the Practice
- The growth and stability of the Practice
- Cashflow
- Profit

Each of the above have great significance within General Practice and the balance maintained between them will shape the future worth of the Practice.

The Main Business Components

The information used to assess the key issues that affect the Practice finances is drawn from three main accountancy items:

- The Balance Sheet
- The Profit and Loss Account
- The Cashflow Statement

Now would be a good time to question how often the above information is available. Some practices only have accounts to satisfy the Inland Revenue requirements, which are invariably produced well after the period in question and can be in arrears. However, there are many wise practices who use their accountants in assisting them to develop internal controls and procedures that will allow good data to be produced to facilitate the production of interim or management accounts. Indeed with the advent of computerisation in General Practice, it is possible to produce the required information daily and therefore allow the ratio models to be even more sensitive.

The Balance Sheet

This is the key document as far as measuring overall profit is concerned. Is the treasure chest full of riches or is it empty? The profit achieved measured against the assets of the Practice together with the funds related to those assets are revealed as a 'snapshot' of time through the production of a Balance Sheet. Regular 'snapshots' are required to see the changes over time.

The Profit and Loss (P&L) Account

This type of reporting is linked to the day-to-day operations of the Practice and the overall profit or loss is determined as either a surplus of income over expenditure or a deficit. Annual accounting principles determine that annual accounts are normally drawn up to represent a 12-month period, with the resulting profit or loss reflected in a Balance Sheet of the same date as the year end. As with the Balance Sheet, the Profit and Loss Account can be produced at a variety of intervals and the results used accordingly.

The Cashflow Statement

This is a very powerful document for business. Even though a practice may make an overall profit, this profit may have been diminished by poor cashflow management. Cashflow is dependent on money being received by the Practice and the timing of money flowing out of the Practice. The reimbursement cycle of General Practice means that there is naturally a quarterly cycle produced as far as cash inputs are concerned, although there is a greater tendency for monthly payments to be received for a larger number of claims. Even so, poor management of the peaks and troughs of General Practice could mean the Practice being disadvantaged in the longer term.

The Ratios

The following ratios may be extracted by taking figures from the balance sheet. By comparing the results of the ratios on a regular basis, it is possible to create a benchmark to identify the profitability of the practice.

Total Assets (TA)

The total assets of the business can be calculated as follows:

Fixed Assets (FA) + Current Assets (CA) = Total Assets (TA)

or alternatively as follows:

Operational Funds (OF) + Long-term Loans (LTL)
+ Current Liabilities (CL) = TA

Whichever method is used, the key factor is the Total Assets (TA) derived.

Your Accountant and Understanding your Accounts

Capital Employed (CE)

Again this ratio can be achieved in two ways:

Fixed Assets (FA) + Current Assets (CA) - Current Liabilities (CL) = CE

or alternatively;

Operational Funds (OF) + Long-term Liabilities (LTL) = CE

Net Worth

This is defined as follows:

Fixed Assets (FA) + Current Assets (CA) - Current Liabilities (CL) - Long-term Liabilities (LTL) = Net Worth (NW)

Working Capital

This is defined as follows:

Current Assets (CA) - Current Liabilities (CL) = Working Capital (WC)

The resultant figure is representative of the liquidity of the practice or in other words the real cash available at a given time.

The above ratios are all derived from the Balance Sheet of the Practice.

Terms Derived from the P&L Account

The previous Balance Sheet ratios are derived from balances on a certain date. The following definitions explain how you determine exactly the amount that you can retain tax-free (ie: your disposable income).

The following terms are derived from the Profit and Loss Account.

Profit before interest and taxation   PBIT

    Less interest =

Profit before taxation   PBT

    Less taxation =

Profit after tax   PAT

    Less drawings =

Retained earnings   RE

111

The Overall Operating Performance of the Practice

The above terms identified from the Profit and Loss Account can be used with the Ratios already identified in the Balance Sheet to provide us with the formulae required to produce an analysis of the Practice accounts. On their own the Ratios and terms can provide specific information about the Practice at a given time, however, when combined and viewed consistently over a period of time, it is possible to measure performance output.

When looking at all the possible combinations of values from the Profit and Loss Account and the Balance Sheet, it is possible to derive a number of formulae. The following are considered appropriate when considering the measurement of performance within General Practice:

Return on Total Assets

This is derived as follows:

Profit before interest and taxation (PBIT) divided by Total Assets (TA) multiplied by 100 to give a percentage value.

Return on Equity

This is derived as follows:

Profit after taxation (PAT) divided by Net Worth (NW) multiplied by 100 to give a percentage value.

Using the Balance Sheet and Profit and Loss Account to Analyse the Financial Health of the Practice

All of the above ratios and formulae need to be looked at in conjunction with actual numbers to assist in deriving their meaning and worth to the reader. By using the example of a Profit and Loss Account (please see page 104) and the example Balance Sheet for our fictional Dr Profitt (please see page 105) we can analyse the financial health of the Practice in the following way:

2002:

First let us look at the performance for the year ended 2002. The ratios and formulae would be applied as follows:

Balance Sheet

Total Assets (TA)

£29,500 + £1,200 = £30,700

or alternatively

£23,948 + £0 + £6,752 = £30,700

Capital Employed (CE)

£29,500 + £1,200 - £6,752 = £23,948

or alternatively

£23,948 + £0 = £23,948

Net Worth

£29,500 + £1,200 - £6,752 - £0 = £23,948

Working Capital

£1,200 - £6,752 = (£5,552)

The Profit and Loss Account

PBIT = £33,259

PBT = £33,259   There is no interest

PAT = £29,259   Taxation shown as £4,000

RE = (£5,552)   Drawings shown as £34,811

Combined Analysis

Return on Total Assets (ROTA)

£33,259 ÷ £30,700 x 100 = 108%

Return on Equity (ROE)

£29,259 ÷ £23,948 x 100 = 122%

2003:

Now let us look at the performance for the year ended 2003. The ratios and formulae would be applied as follows;

Balance Sheet

Total Assets (TA)

£29,500 + £1,035 = £30,535

or alternatively

£25,983 + £0 + £4,552 = £30,535

Capital Employed (CE)

£29,500 + £1,035 - £4,552 = £25,983

or alternatively

£25,983 + £0 = £25,983

Net Worth

£29,500 + £1,035 - £4,552 - £0 = £25,983

Working Capital

£1,035 - £4,552 = (£3,517)

The Profit and Loss Account

PBIT = £41,535

PBT = £41,535   There is no interest

PAT = £37,035   Taxation shown as £4,500

RE = £2,035   Drawings shown as £35,000

Combined Analysis

Return on Total Assets (ROTA)

£41,535 ÷ £30,535 x 100 = 136%

Return on Equity (ROE)

£37,035 ÷ £25,983 x 100 = 142%

Two-Year Analysis

Having analysed the results of both years' data, it is possible to compare the statistics to demonstrate whether the practice is improving or weakening financially:

Total Assets	2002 =	£30,700	2003 =	£ 30,535
Capital Employed	2002 =	£23,948	2003 =	£25,983
Net Worth	2002 =	£23,948	2003 =	£25,983
Working Capital	2002 =	(£5,552)	2003 =	(£3,517)
PBIT	2002 =	£33,259	2003 =	£41,535
PBT	2002 =	£33,259	2003 =	£41,535
PAT	2002 =	£29,259	2003 =	£37,035
RE	2002 =	(£5,552)	2003 =	£2,035
ROTA	2002 =	108%	2003 =	136%
ROE	2002 =	122%	2003 =	142%

It is clear that the Practice is in a stronger position in 2003 than in 2002. However, whilst it has been able to clear its bank overdraft and increase its profits, the overall liquidity of the Practice is still fragile. In other words, if it had to pay all its creditors tomorrow, it would need a new bank facility or an injection of capital from the doctor.

The liquidity of the Practice would be improved if the working capital could be converted to a positive figure. This could be achieved by the doctor reducing his level of drawings accordingly. This in turn would lead to there being a greater amount of money in the bank higher or a reduction in the level of creditors if money was subsequently spent.

The main point about the use of Ratios is to help inform management decisions and to act as catalyst for change by providing an early warning system of changes to the financial make-up of the Practice. By analysing trends and looking at the consistency of the Practice performance, effective planning can be achieved to help maximise the longer-term profitability of the Practice.

Relationships with Others

Having seen how financial performance measures may be utilised and how the basis of accounts are drawn up, we now need to consider the relationships that the Practice has with outside agencies and how the analysis of the financial situation might be used.

The PCT

Primarily the PCT will determine the allocations given to GPs in respect of their new GMS or existing PMS Contract. Therefore, it is important to be able to demonstrate to the Primary Care Trust that the Contract value being received is commensurate with the level of work being completed. Statistics concerning the actual number of cases or visits being made will help this scenario. The PCT will look for significant contract variations or exceptional circumstances. Understanding your accounts and being able to analyse key ratios will assist in preparing your financial argument accordingly.

The Accountant

Your accountant will need to be briefed on any anomalies contained within Local Contract Agreements. For example, if a practice receives contract income for the employment of a salaried GP, but does not recruit immediately, the accounting treatment of this sum may be dealt with differently to reduce any unnecessary liability to tax. Also by allowing the accountant enough time to produce your accounts, you will be able to look at other factors that could also assist in reducing your fees and overall tax liability.

Financial Advisors

Most financial advisors will be looking to raise finance on existing equity or looking to maximise investments. It is worth remembering that it is often the presentation of information that helps lenders make relevant decisions. Very often, taking a little extra time to provide illustrations or explanations will help secure that particular financial deal. There are still lenders who ask questions such as "Do you consider that this business or individual will continue to receive the same level of turnover?" The reason for this is that most organisations do not treat GPs any differently from any other individual or commercial organisation. However, for most GP practices, their level of income (turnover) is determined by the contract under which they operate.

The Practice needs to understand the science of accounting in order to appreciate the art of good accounting and the ways in which it can secure profitability and long-term financial stability.

CHAPTER 9

MAXIMISING PROFIT
IN PRACTICE

If you take into consideration the items covered in the previous chapters, it becomes clear that maximising profit is not just about money and finances. It is about a clear understanding of the contractual framework of the relevant GP Contract and subsequently a sound interpretation of the same. At the same time it is important to link this with the enabling legislation that controls the way in which income is assessed and taxed by the Inland Revenue. This chapter outlines some of the practical ways of always ensuring that this can be done.

Tax Payments

For most GP Practices with a year end at 31st March, the Accounts to 31st March 2003 will determine the tax liability for the 2002/03 tax year ending on the 5th April 2003. In order to assess the liability to tax, it will be necessary to produce the accounts as quickly as possible after the year end. Often in practice, there can be delays in providing information but this is not usually a problem if the profits are consistent because it is possible to plan on the basis that the taxation costs will be roughly the same as in previous years. Where profits rise, there will be an increased balancing payment, with an increased payment on account, giving a double tax blow. Conversely, if profits fall, there may be a possibility for a tax rebate and a reduction to the next payment on account if it is actioned before 31st July 2003.

Prior to the introduction of the Self-Assessment rules in 1997, a number of Practices had a year end close to 30th June, and for a Practice which has retained that year end, the Accounts to 30th June 2002 will determine the 2002/03 tax liability.

The New Partner or Partnership

A GP in practice in 2001/02 with a year ending 30th June will be required to make 2002/03 Payments on Account (PoA) on 31st January 2003 and 31st July 2003, but a new Partner is unlikely to have made any PoAs. Therefore, it is important that there is a clear understanding that there will be a tax liability for the new Partner for the profits earned from the time when the new Partner starts. The balance of the 2002/03 tax liability becomes due by 31st January 2004, and at the same time the first 2003/04 PoA also becomes due, a particular problem for new Partners. If in doubt, ensure that a tax provision is made for all earnings from commencement with the Practice: put aside an amount of money with which to pay the tax – and you can also earn interest on that money in the meantime

Given that the GPs in the Practice will be paying half of the next year's tax on 31st January, if the taxable income increases, this typically gives rise to 40% extra tax for 2002/03, and an increase in the 2003/04 PoA of 20%. While the top tax rate remains at 40%, both of these are payable in January 2004 which means the tax payments will increase by 60% of the increase in income. With the introduction of the PMS Contract and the new GMS contract, GP salaries have been showing a marked increase. Very often these increases are linked to the contractual sum and consideration should be given to potential tax liabilities as soon as the contract value is known at the beginning of the tax year.

Since 1997, tax bills have been personal liabilities but early warning of tax liabilities and a tax reserve retained in the Practice account can still prevent a cashflow problem. As already discussed, early knowledge of the potential tax liability will help to prevent cashflow problems, particularly in January. Care should also be taken about paying all tax through the Partnership account, particularly where a GP earns considerable income from outside of the Practice. Only the proportion of tax that relates to the Partnership should be paid by the whole Practice. Any GP who has another income from outside the practice should make necessary provision for the taxation on this sum.

Tax After Retirement

A doctor who retires on 31st March 2003 will have made a 2002/03 PoA on 31st January 2003, but will still have a PoA due on 31st July 2003 and a balancing payment due 31st January 2004. This outstanding liability is often overlooked and comes as an unwelcome surprise. Always remember that part of all Self-Assessment tax liabilities are paid after the tax year in which the income is earned or received. Therefore, tax planning is particularly vital should a GP plan to retire or even leave a practice to carry on other work.

The Inland Revenue

The Collector of Taxes was given a new remit in April 2001 and now has a more aggressive approach to tax collection, nationally and locally. Legislation has been introduced that empowers inspectors to seek information earlier or to impose penalties for late submission. They can also ask for more information from the taxpayer directly. It is important to make tax payments when they fall due! Our own experience is that doctors are as likely to be targeted as any other business. Under Self-Assessment the Inland Revenue have powers to investigate Tax Returns at random, although most investigations are the result of unusual figures.

It is possible to obtain tax investigation insurance. It is important to read the policy details carefully – there are a normally a number of exclusion clauses. You should remember it is not the accountant's fault if your practice is investigated, but often it will mean that your accountant will need to do extra work to ensure that the investigation is satisfactorily closed. In general, good records and supporting evidence will result in an investigation quickly being brought to a close.

Problem Areas

The Inspector of Taxes looks particularly closely at any cash transactions and estimates. GPs should have an effective method of recording all cash income, in particular any passport signing fees or cleaning fees or casual staff payments. As well as any estimated expenses, estimates of private mileage or high estimates of business use of home phone attract attention. The Practice should record all business mileage using a form and should retain receipts for motoring expenses/travel expenses. The business proportion of mileage has reduced dramatically where alternative transport is used. The Inland Revenue are aware of this!

Accounts and Fees

Every well-managed business strives to keep costs down and one cost that they may be able to reduce is the fees that they pay to their accountants. Accountants' fees vary and are primarily based on the time required to produce the Accounts. Providing the accountants with detailed, well-maintained records can prove to be very cost-effective in reducing the fees. Remember that, you do not necessarily need the services of the accountant to produce your accounts, but, if you are going to use an accountant, it may help you to reduce costs if you consider providing the following items when you submit your records and vouchers next time:

- An analysed cash book of Practice Income (or computer equivalent)

- Supporting schedules of NHS fees, reimbursements, and other income or contract details in the case of PMS

- An analysed cash book of Practice Expenses (or computer equivalent)

- Documentation in support of expenses

- A reconciliation of the cash book balance with the bank statements

- Petty cash records (if any) or a petty cash day book showing relevant spending.

- Details of amounts owed to the Practice at the year end (including schedules of fees received later)
  These are known as your debtors.

- Details of amounts owed by the Practice at the year end. These are known as your creditors.

Generally records which are written up continuously throughout the year are significantly more accurate than those written up occasionally (or, in extreme cases, once per year). Details of individual GPs' personal expense claims are sometimes not readily available. Since these have to be included in the Partnership Tax Return this delays submitting the Returns of all the Partners. It is important to be able to substantiate the expense claims in respect of home telephones, mobile phones, books, education and other items. If this is not done, then it will delay the whole process. In the event of a large practice partnership, this can cause problems and therefore some practices elect to show separately those business expenses that are paid privately or to offset them against other income for example, an income from private practice. With the flexibility being introduced by the new GMS Contract, serious consideration will need to be given to both income and expenses outside the Practice and how these are accounted.

Limited Companies

Where a practice has a significant non-NHS income, there can be a tax saving by routing this through a limited company. If this is done, it is important that completely separate records are maintained, and appropriate expenses correctly allocated.

If a GP has a significant non-NHS income, then he or she could consider the use of a limited company to obtain tax advantages, such as drawing of director's dividends. This will attract taxation at 10%, with the appropriate tax credit being available to the recipient. Also there are tax advantages in respect of when the tax is due. A limited company could be used to act as an investment company to own assets such as property and then rent back the premises to the Practice. This option is already used by some GPs under the PMS Contracts but could prove to be more popular under the new GMS rules.

The down side to limited companies are that they are statutory bodies and certain documentation must be filed on time or the Company faces the risk of fines or penalties.

Pension Contributions

Those employees of hospitals and other members of the employed service NHS pension scheme receive 1/80th of final salary for each year of employment and therefore after forty years will have 50% of final salary plus tax free lump sum of three times that amount. This can include GPs with hospital appointments.

General Practitioners generally contribute to a separate NHS pension scheme. Under the new Contract, this is one area where pay can be deemed eligible for superannuation in the year before it is actually earned. Typical superannuable earnings of £50,000 at the contribution rate of 6% gives an annual contribution rate of £3,000. Over a period of forty years, this generates a pension of £25,000 per annum plus £75,000 tax-free lump sum. It is unusual to achieve 40 working years, so GPs can buy added years. If the usual 6% contribution funds say 36 years, the pro rata contribution rate for another 4 years would be an added 0.67% in total. The actual contribution rate required is 1.09% for each year, and other alternatives should be considered. In certain circumstances it is possible to stop buying added years. Buying additional years can cause a problem in a partnership, particularly if the Additional Voluntary Contributions are being deducted at source by the PCT making payments. Very often it may lead to full superannuation contributions being overstated in respect of the Partnership.

Because of the way the NHS scheme works, the first year superannuable income of a GP is vital. New GPs should try to achieve a full profit share in the first year even if it means making a capital payment to the other partners in order to receive a greater share of the Practice profits. Contributions under the new scheme will fund a pension of approximately 50% of final salary in retirement. This is reduced by 25% for retirement at age 55, or by 40% at age 50. A GP retiring at 60 will find he or she has more leisure time than previously, and only half the income. There may be non-superannuable earnings that, after deducting expenses, may permit a Personal or Stakeholder Pension contribution to be paid. This is an investment and the proceeds are only limited by the investment performance, not by the final salary. With the current rules on such pension schemes the GP would only need an income on which the contributions are made in the first year. Contributions could continue for a further five years at the same rate, even though the pensionable earnings may be less. This means that it may be possible to plan for retirement at age 65, but only work as hard for one of the five remaining years. This can be achieved by making the most of other disposable income, which may have been invested in other areas, but yielding a lower aggregate return.

Stakeholder Pensions

Although intended for employees who would not normally contribute to a pension scheme, Stakeholder schemes can be applicable to a GP (as discussed) and also for a spouse, children or grandchildren. Even for a non-working spouse or child, contributions up to £2,808 can be made and will attract a tax relief contribution of £792. With the introduction of PMS and the new GMS Contract, it should be easier to take advantage of spouses' salary, where relief is not being claimed elsewhere.

Cost Rent and Notional Rent Calculations

The Cost Rent Scheme was introduced in the 1970s. It allows GPs to acquire a valuable capital investment, such as a surgery, without a heavy capital outlay. However, the rules became more restrictive in the early 1990s, but even so the advantages still remained. A GP is eligible for the reimbursement of the rent and rates relating to the surgery premises. Rather than accepting the reimbursement at the current market rate (also known as the notional rent), they may apply for reimbursement relating to the cost of providing separate purpose-built premises or its equivalent (the cost rent). To qualify for cost rent, the GP must either build new premises or buy premises for substantial modification or substantially modify existing premises.

The allowable costs under a cost rent scheme are largely fixed by Health Authority criteria but are affected by a location factor based upon the Building Cost Information Service (BCIS) annual figures for local differences.

If a practice intends to build new premises, it can be important to get agreement from the District Valuer (DV) as to the value of a green or brown field site before any proposals are put forward as DVs have been known to quote different values for the same site. Indeed, the Inland Revenue would probably value any such site for inheritance purposes at far higher value. Do seek advice from the DV. Quite often the DV will be able to make suggestions for ways in which the valuation can be legitimately increased (for example, through enabling the building to be used by more patients).

DVs operate in their own individual areas and are not truly independent so their suggested notional rent should not be accepted without careful consideration. It can be worthwhile to consult a qualified Chartered Surveyor to agree the notional rent. There are specialist firms of surveyors who have experience of negotiating across the country. Obtaining this information, before the visit of the DV is quite important. If valuations are even slightly adrift from the current market or costs, then this can have a severe impact on the Practice for up to three years. The decision to change from cost rent to notional rent will depend upon the notional rent that can be negotiated with the DV and is a one-way decision. Technically the notional rent assessment is based upon a theoretical fifteen year term with three yearly upward only rent reviews, internal repairing only, vacant and to let, exclusive of rates and with a right to assign. The assumption is made that other suitable planning permission would be available. If you are not sure, then take your time to consider all the options and do not make an irreversible decision.

Personal or Business Borrowing

The recently introduced, all-in-one personal accounts are particularly attractive to higher rate taxpayers and become even more so when there is disposable income available. All-in-one personal accounts pool interest and savings in one account and offsets these against the outstanding liability or mortgage. This means that you could be saving considerable interest charges over a 25-year period. (These savings could amount to as much as tens of thousands on an average mortgage!)

Where tax relief is not available on borrowings, (for example, as with a domestic mortgage), reducing the interest paid will generate a much higher rate of return than interest received net of higher rate tax on savings. If money is invested in an ordinary savings account it will be taxed at basic rate and therefore there will be an additional sum of tax to pay to the higher rate. If this money was invested in a single all-in-one account, the interest overall would be reduced and a saving would be created over the term of the mortgage rather than additional tax being due. Where the opportunity exists, a domestic mortgage or other borrowing should be paid off as quickly as possible in preference to repaying a loan to acquire surgery premises which qualifies for tax relief, normally at 40%.

Many GPs do not realise that their most important asset is their freehold surgery and therefore this should be regarded as a positive source for raising finance and relief can be obtained for a qualifying loan. GPs can be guilty of borrowing too much and it is not unknown for the insolvency of doctors to occur. Appropriate advice should be sought when raising personal finance from an independent financial advisor.

Recently, there has been bad press about the performance of endowment policies. If you hold an endowment policy, it can be informative to write to the insurance company and ask for three values:

- The Surrender Value

- The Paid-up Maturity Value and

- The Expected Maturity Value if premiums continue at their current rate.

It may be that the policy is no longer going to yield the expected outcome. If it seems that the policy is a poor investment and you decide not to continue the policy, it will be necessary to consider replacing the life insurance cover before the policy is cancelled. This may be available from the same insurance company, although it is usually worth 'shopping around'.

GPs should consider their potential Inheritance Tax and take appropriate steps. The Inheritance Tax threshold is now £255,000 – and Inheritance Tax is paid at 40%. GPs should have a Will and probably life policies written in trust. A nil rate band discretionary trust will generally be appropriate for most GPs. Older GPs should consider using the annual gift exemptions. To avoid paying any inheritance tax, provision should be made within 7 years of death for lifetime transfers. The gift allowance is a way of transferring goods and money to dependents on an annual basis.

Partnership Agreements

Partnership Agreements should be updated on a regular basis, in order that there is no room for error if things go wrong. (Further information appears in Annex A). When a partnership works, agreements do not seem necessary. When there is a partnership dissolution, a well-written Partnership Agreement proves to be well-worth the cost of preparing one.

A Partnership Agreement should generally provide for health cover after one month of illness. Generally, GPs have a good sickness record but the Partnership Agreement should include provision for cases of genuine long-term sickness. In case long-term illness leads to an inability to work, it is advisable for the Partnership Agreements to provide permanent health insurance to take effect after 12 months of illness. By not claiming tax relief on the permanent health insurance policy premiums, the proceeds of the policy are tax-free. Such health insurance arrangements should allow an amount to cover any loan repayments if there is borrowing for surgery premises.

With the introduction of PMS, some new partners are sometimes reluctant to purchase into surgery premises at cost rent values and Partnership Agreements should cover the replacement of a retiring partner's interest in the property, taking into account the Capital Gains Tax taper relief rules. The original Capital Gains Tax (CGT) was introduced in 1965 in order to tax the gains made on disposals of capital assets. Indexation relief was introduced to ensure that actual gains, rather than just monetary gains, are taxed. Chargeable gains are taxed at the higher rate less the annual capital gains tax relief. The sale of the asset share of the surgery is the most likely to attract CGT. However, the taper relief available will minimise the amount of tax due. Also obtaining finance or working capital (perhaps through a loan secured against the practice surgery) are also tax efficient ways of making the Practice assets work harder for the finances of the Practice. Partnership Agreements will generally need to be reconsidered in respect of profit sharing on transfer to PMS or the new GMS Contract.

Employed or Self-Employed?

GPs are very defensive, and quite rightly so, of their self-employed status. Under PMS there is the option to be employed or self-employed. It is necessary to bear in mind that the self-employed get deductions for expenses 'wholly and exclusively' incurred for the purpose of the business whereas employees only get deductions for expenses 'wholly, exclusively and necessarily' incurred. The extra word, 'necessarily' means that training courses are only tax deductible if paid for by the employer. The only normal expense of a GP who is an employee (under the PAYE scheme) would be their subscriptions. A GP who is self-employed can take part of the ownership of the surgery and this can be a worthwhile investment and attract business asset Capital Gains Tax taper relief. Self-employment provides the opportunity for greater tax planning and flexibility. PAYE is more restrictive, although can be less stressful, without the need for annual tax returns and potential penalties or investigations.

The New GMS Contract: Action Required

At the time of writing, the new GMS Contract had been delayed and full information was not yet available. It is suggested that the direct contract with the Secretary of State will no longer apply. Instead, the new GMS Contracts will be a contract with the PCT – and thus have a local emphasis. There will be a Practice-based contract with patients effectively worth an amount of money. There will be some adjustment for deprived and rural areas. There may not be seniority payments, reimbursement of staff and possibly no need for an earnings review body. Therefore, negotiating the best deal is of paramount importance.

The BMA are keen to negotiate for a national contract but with local variations. The BMA do not have a say in the type of detail included under PMS contracts.

The new contracts will involve a lot of business planning and the need to be forward-looking and, even more importantly, acutely aware of local needs and local opportunities. This could include income from certain private fees and will require an awareness of the amount of time needed to earn a certain level of income. Even more importantly, it will be necessary for GPs to calculate their most profitable and least profitable working hours. Partnership Agreements (see Annex A) will need to be varied to reflect the new Contracts and to divide profits in an appropriate way, much more akin to commercial arrangements for other professionals.

Update on the new GMS Contract (Summer 2003)

In June 2003 (just before this book went to press) GPs voted by ballot to accept the new GMS Contract. This acceptance followed the clarification of certain issues, notably:

- The ways in which the allocation formula would be applied
- The removal of the 100/150 quality points criteria for practices requiring the Minimum Practice Guarantee
- The need to maintain incentives to improve quality
- The introduction of disease prevalence as a basis for weighting quality payments
- The local appeal mechanism for seniority payments
- The implications for practices currently operating under the PMS Contracts (including confirmation from the Department of Health that PMS practices would receive the same level of new investment as GMS practices).

It is now vital that all GP practices (particularly those that are PMS) assess their current status, plan for the future and explore potential financial opportunities.

ANNEX A:
THE PARTNERSHIP AGREEMENT

Why Have a Partnership Deed?

We have all heard about partnerships that have split up without managing to reach a mutually satisfactory arrangement – leaving one or more of the doctors feeling bitter and, perhaps, out of pocket. It is one of those situations that all GPs fear but it is also one of those things that we tend to think will happen to other people but not us.

In fact there is the potential for any partnership to break up (even if everything seems to have worked well for many years). If a break up does happen, the absence of a partnership deed often simply compounds the anguish of an already very difficult scenario.

The purpose of this annex is to describe the nature of partnership agreements and to help GPs to formulate partnership agreements that should cover all eventualities – and could save them from a lot of anguish in the future.

Whilst it may be acceptable to have a gentleman's agreement in the absence of a formal deed, it could be this lack of formal documentation that could potentially cost the Practice dearly in the future. It can be argued that many practices have survived quite successfully in the past without such an agreement but, in the event that a dispute did arise, the absence of an agreement would only prolong the likely resolution of the matter and would likely involve the incurring of increased legal and accountancy costs. This expense is not only unnecessary but also avoidable if partnership agreements are periodically reviewed and updated and agreed by all partners.

The deed is not designed to act as a constraint, but to assist when problems do arise. Therefore it should be written not because there are problems within the practice, but as a prudent measure to facilitate resolutions to any problems that arise in the future. Seeking correct legal advice at the beginning of a partnership could prove to be more cost-effective than having to suffer the legal costs of a drawn out partnership dispute at a much later date. This form of agreement could also be applicable to single-handed practitioners who may in the future find the need to work more in collaboration with other practices.

What Happens if there is No Partnership Agreement?

Surprisingly, where no written or verbal agreement exists, there is a statute requirement that dates back to the 1890 Partnership Act which identifies the rights and obligations of partners. In the absence of a partnership agreement or where an internal dispute has arisen, the legal process, namely the courts will look to this act to determine such rights and obligations and will hence judge how they perceive the partnership should be conducting its partnership affairs.

The Act is made up of a number of sections with sections relating to the relationships of partners to one another being covered by sections 19 to 31. Section 24 of the 1890 Act details specific interests and obligations of partners. In essence, the interest of partners in the practice property (assets) and their respective obligations will be determined subject to any written or expressed agreement in place by the partners by the following key rulings:

- All partners will equally share in the capital (assets) and profits of the Practice (business) and equally each partner will contribute to losses, whether capital or otherwise

- Each partner must be indemnified in respect of payments made by him and in respect of any personal liabilities incurred by him in connection with the general running of the Practice

- A partner who makes a payment or advance in excess of the agreed capital contribution will be entitled to interest at a rate of an agreed percentage per annum with effect from the date of the payment

- Not withstanding the above, the partners are not entitled to receive interest on capital subscribed before profits are determined

- Each partner is entitled to manage equally and take an active part in the business

- No remuneration is payable for someone acting in the partnership business

- No new partner may be introduced unless prior approval is given by all existing partners

- General matters concerning the day-to-day running of the business may be made by a majority of the partners, but matters affecting the partnership agreement must be made by all partners

- The partnership records should be kept at the place of business and must be accessible for inspection by any of the partners at any time thought to be necessary.

Given the above, it appears clearly that the conditions of the 1890 Act are sufficiently explicit to afford a degree of assurance to any member of the Practice. However, the partners of the practice are free to reach a formal agreement amongst themselves which can incorporate some or all of the above plus include other specific requirements that depart from the rules quoted above.

What Should be Included in The Agreement?

Given the scenario that an agreement does exist, what should be included and what should be excluded from such an agreement? A partnership agreement can vary from practice to practice and can include exhaustive lists of requirements and obligations. The following is an example model of a partnership deed. Where appropriate commentary is annotated.

An Example of a Partnership Agreement

PARTNERSHIP DEED

AN AGREEMENT made this —— day of —— Two Thousand and —— —— between,

* —— of —— and,

* —— of —— and,

* —— of ——

IT IS HEREBY AGREED AND DECLARED AS FOLLOWS;

The said *, *, and *, shall become and remain partners in the business of General Practice for a term of —— years from the date of this deed if they shall so long live.

Commentary: commercial partnerships are often of limited duration, but General Practice by its nature is often deemed to carry on indefinitely. If partners anticipate that a partnership will dissolve within a given time frame it could lead to competition developing amongst themselves rather than working for the business.

Although the partnership constituted by this deed is for a period of —— years nevertheless it is the intention of all the parties hereto to continue in partnership from —— year period to —— year period subject only to the incidence of death or retirement.

Commentary: If a fixed term agreement is reached, there should be provision included for it to be continued on the same terms on expiry of the fixed term.

The death, retirement, expulsion or bankruptcy of a partner shall not determine the partnership between the partners but without prejudice to the generality of this clause the parties hereto shall review the provisions of this deed whenever the admission of a new profit-sharing partner into the partnership is being contemplated.

Commentary: It is important to include a clause that ensures, say on death of a partner, that an automatic dissolution of partnership does not take place between existing partners as a result of such a clause being omitted. In General Practice, a good deed will ensure that the duration of the agreement will continue during the joint lives of at least two of the remaining partners, who were party to the agreement. General dissolution can be effected at any time by general consent amongst the partners.

The partners shall practise in partnership under the name of —— (or such other name as the partners may hereafter agree). The business shall be carried out at the main surgery located at —— and the branch surgery located at ——.

Commentary: In general most GPs will use their own names under which to practise. However, when a business name other than their true name is used, it is a requirement of the 1985 Business Names Act to ensure that all partners names appear on the practice correspondence.

The bankers of the practice shall be —— Bank PLC or such bankers as the partners shall agree upon both for practice and private income attributable to the members of the partnership.

All partnership money shall be paid to the bankers of the partnership to the credit of the partnership and the partners shall make such regulations as they may from time to time see fit for operating or closing the bank accounts of the partnership and for providing the money required for current expenses.

All outgoings incurred for or in carrying on the practice business and all losses and damages which shall happen or be incurred in relation to the practice are to be paid out of monies and profits of the partnership and if there is a deficiency shall be contributed by the partners in the shares in which they are, for the time being, respectively entitled to the profits of the partnership.

Commentary: The banking regulations agreed upon will normally allow any of the partners to sign cheques, but normally any cheques in excess of a predetermined limit should always require a counter-signature from one or other partners.

The initial capital of the practice shall be a sum equal to £x to be contributed by the partners in equal shares together with further such cash capital (if any) as the partners may from time to time agree to be required (in addition to any loan capital) for the purposes of the practice and which shall be provided (except as may from time to time be otherwise agreed by the partners) in the proportion in which the partners are for the time being entitled to share in the profits of the partnership.

Commentary: It is important for an incoming partner to review the basis of the capital share of the Practice, because this will cause potential tax implications if not fully understood and very often not all the capital assets are equitably assigned. If no provision is made in the deed to allow interest to be payable on capital introduced, there will be none payable.

The partners shall be entitled to the net profits arising from the practice in equal share or such other shares as may from time to time be agreed by the partners.

Commentary: It is vitally important that if all income is not to be equally distributed that a provision is made that the profit share for tax purposes is determined subject to adjustments for income and expenditure attributable to individual partners.

The control and management of the practice shall remain in the hands of the partners and salaried partners (if any) shall not be entitled to take part therein.

All agendas and minutes of partner's meeting and balance sheets and profit and loss accounts shall be circulated to all partners.

On xx/xx/xx and on the same day in each succeeding year the accounts of the practice shall be made up. Each partner may draw on account of his share of profit to such extent as may be decided by the partners from time to time.

Commentary: Good management control on finances can be achieved if partners drawings are regularly reviewed and linked with practice profit and cashflow.

Each partner shall diligently employ himself or herself in the partnership business and carry on and conduct the same for the greatest advantage of the practice. Each partner shall be entitled to x weeks holiday in aggregate in each year of the partnership.

Commentary: It should be clearly stipulated how many days a year holiday entitlement there is for each partner and whether arrangements are permissible for sabbatical activities and whether there are any restrictions as to when annual holiday may be taken.

No partner shall without the previous consent of the others:

- employ or dismiss any employee or take on any trainee
- purchase goods in the name or on behalf of the practice to an amount exceeding £x
- compound, release or discharge any debt owing to the partnership without receiving the amount therefor
- be engaged or interested whether directly or indirectly in any business or occupation other than the practice business
- advance the moneys of or deliver on credit any goods belonging to the partnership
- make any assignment either absolutely or by way of a charge of his share in the partnership
- give any security or undertaking for the payment of any debt or liability out of the monies or property of the partnership
- introduce or attempt to introduce, without prior agreement, another person into the practice partnership
- enter into any bond or become surety for any persons or do so knowingly permit to be done anything whereby the capital or property of the partnership may be seized, attached or taken in execution.

Commentary: It is generally unwise to have a very large number of prohibitions, because this could restrict the activities of the practice unduly. However, they do provide for dissolution of the practice if a practice partner is in wilful or persistent breach of them or the partnership agreement in general.

Every Partner shall during the partnership pay his present and future separate debts and at all times indemnify the other partners and each of them and the capital and effects of the partnership against his said debts and engagements and against all actions, suits, claims and demands on account thereof.

If any partner shall:

- by act or default commit any flagrant breach of his duties as a partner or of the agreements and stipulations herein contained, or

- fail to account and pay over or refund to the partnership any money for which he is accountable to the partnership within 14 days after being required to do so by a partner specifically so authorised by a decision of the partners, or

- act in any respect contrary to the good faith which ought to be observed between partners, or

- become subject to the bankruptcy laws, or

- enter into any composition or arrangement with or for the benefit of his creditors, or

- be or become permanently incapacitated by ill health, accident or otherwise from attending to practice business, or

- except with the consent of the other partners, absent himself from the practice for more than X calendar months in any one year or for more than X consecutive days (absence during the usual holidays or due to temporary illness or as agreed not being reckoned)

then in any such case above, the other partners may by notice in writing given to him or other appropriate person or left at the offices of the partnership determine the partnership so far as he may be concerned and publish a notice of dissolution of the partnership in the name of and as against such partner whereupon the partnership will so far as regards such partner immediately cease and determine accordingly but without prejudice to the remedies of the other partners for any antecedent breach of any of the stipulations or agreements aforesaid any question as to a case having arisen to authorise such notice shall be referred to arbitration.

Upon the dissolution of the partnership by the death of a partner or by a partner retiring, the other partners shall be entitled to purchase upon the terms hereinafter specified the share of the partner so dying or retiring: provided that written notice of intention to purchase shall be given to the retiring partner or to the personal representatives of the deceased partners within X calendar months after the date of the dissolution.

The purchase money payable under the above paragraph hereof shall be the net value of the share of the deceased or retiring partner as at the date of the dissolution after satisfying all outstanding liabilities of the partnership with interest at the rate of X% per annum as from the date of dissolution: provided that if the value of the said share cannot be agreed upon the same shall be submitted to arbitration in the manner hereinafter provided.

The purchase money shall be paid by X equal instalments, the first instalment to be paid at the end of X months after the date of dissolution and thereafter at the end of each succeeding period of X months with interest at the rate of X% per annum upon so much of the purchase money as shall remain unpaid for the time being and such purchase money shall if required be secured by the bond of the surviving partners with not fewer than two sureties.

In the event of one of the partners retiring and the other partners purchasing his share the retiring partner shall not during the unexpired residue of the term of the partnership carry on or be interested either directly or indirectly in any business which might affect the practice.

Should any doubt or difference arise at any time between the said partners or their personal representatives with regard to the interpretation or effect of this agreement or in respect of the rights, duties and liabilities of any partner or his personal representatives whether in connection with the conduct or winding up of the affairs of the partnership, such doubt or difference shall be submitted to an arbitrator appointed by the Chairman of [name of town/city] Primary Care Trust.

In witness whereof the parties hereto have hereunto set their hands and seals the day and year first above mentioned.

Commentary: Partnership deeds usually contain various and often complicated provisions relating to issues such as life assurance for retirement, key man insurance, annuities for partners' dependants in the case of death, and annuities to partners in the event of permanent incapacity. There are often, in the case of general practices which are already well established, specific provisions or supplementary clauses relating the payments to be made to a retiring partner or on death and particularly the effects of a continuation election for tax purposes.

Conclusion

The above template of a partnership deed is not exhaustive, but is illustrative of the potential areas of concern should an agreement not be in place. Partnership deeds should not be seen as being restrictive to the Practice. They should be put in place to ensure that matters run smoothly when or if there is a future problem. Too often, partners think about an agreement once the problem has occurred and this is where the potential loss situation occurs. Very often disputing partners will take separate and independent legal and accountancy advice and, as a result, discussions get drawn out over a longer period of time. This will inevitably lead to higher costs and potential tax implications.

In the absence of a partnership agreement, it seems sensible to be aware of the implications concerning partnership law. Where there exists an agreement, it is most prudent to ensure that all clauses are fully understood and, if need be, re-written in terminology which all partners understand and agree to.

Whilst the need for an agreement may not be apparent now, knowing that one exists will ensure that where there is a future problem, it is resolved with the minimum disruption and cost to all involved.

ANNEX B
THE TAX RETURN

Making the Return

The purpose of this Annex is to provide detail about who has to complete a tax return, when it has to be completed and the general rules concerning the completion of tax returns. The rules governing tax returns tend to change fairly regularly. These changes are usually announced in the preceding year's budget. Noting and understanding these changes will help you to avoid unnecessary payments (such as penalties and interest) and will help you to plan how to use available resources cost-effectively.

When an individual receives a return, he or she is obliged to make reply to the Inland Revenue. In the case of most General Practitioners, this requirement is already established and will continue. However, if a return is not received by the Revenue, the taxpayer still has obligations to the Inland Revenue if the individual is liable for income tax and/or capital gains tax unless any of the following apply:

- There are no chargeable gains at all. (All gains including those within current exemption limits must be notified to the Inspector of Taxes).

- All income falls within certain categories and is taxed completely at source.

The return has recently undergone changes that have led to a increase in the size of the return. Further tax legislation may lead to future amendments and the following is a summary of the information available at the time of writing this book and will be updated in future editions.

The return will consist of primarily a certificate by the taxpayer, a list of supporting schedules and the tax calculation (if the taxpayer has not opted for the Revenue to calculate this). The Revenue should only send the schedules that are applicable to the individual and it will be the responsibility of the taxpayer to request further schedules in any given year. For example, if a GP is employed, he may receive an employment schedule, but if he has more than one employer then he will need to complete a separate schedule for each. Each individual module of the return will consist of an individual schedule and its supporting guidance notes. Based on the current return, the modules will consist of the following, although this list may be subject to further amendment.

Q1 Employment

Q2 Share Schemes

Q3 Self-employment

Q4 Partnership

Q5 Land and Property

Q6 Foreign

Q7 Trusts etc

Q8 Capital Gains

Q9 Non-residence

Q10 UK dividends, Stock dividends, Foreign income dividends

Q11 UK Pensions, retirement annuity or Social Security benefits

Q12 Capital Gains on policies etc

Q13 All other UK income

Q14 Relief for Pension Contributions

Q15 Deductions and reliefs

Q16 Blind Persons' allowance, married couples or tax credits

Q17 Student Loan payments

Q18   Student Loan calculations and tax repayments

Q19   Tax repayment claim

Q20   Tax refunded already

Q21   Details

Q22   Personal Details

Q23   Additional Information

Q24   Declaration

The average GP may not ever need to complete all of the above schedules, but may during any given period need to complete at least three to four of the above and from time-to-time additional schedules. Therefore, just because the GP is not sent one of the above schedules it does not remove the obligation on the taxpayer to request further appropriate schedules.

Very often the Practitioner is not involved in the day-to-day record keeping of the Practice and it is often left to a particular GP, who is given overall responsibility for that area. However, given that it is the individual Partner who is held liable, it is important to know which records must be maintained. Therefore anyone making a tax return must retain the appropriate information in support of that claim.

The records of the Practice must include all receipts and expenses and all matters involving the purchase and sale of goods. Supporting documentation must be retained including accounts, books, vouchers, deeds, contracts and receipts. This should not cause too many problems for the well-organised Practice, but there are still many practices where payments are made to GPs, prior to the appropriate documentation being received or where amounts are paid on account and the official documentation is mislaid, leaving records incomplete. General Practice is deemed to be a business and therefore is required to keep records for six years after 31st January following the year of assessment. This does not only apply to the records of the practice but also to the records of the individual taxpayer.

Example:

Dr Profitt is a sole practitioner and employs his wife Mrs Profitt. The Inspector of Taxes carries out an inspection of their returns for the period 1999-00, which is completed by the Inspector on 30/6/2003.

Dr Profitt must keep records until 31st January 2006. Mrs Profitt need only keep records up to 30/6/2003 on the basis that this is the date that any enquiries have been completed.

In general, most returns will be issued by the Inland Revenue during April of the period concerned. This return must be received by the Inspector of Taxes by the following 31st January unless you wish the Inspector to complete the assessment in which case the return must be sent by 30th September (four months earlier). Where a return is issued before 31st July and the taxpayer elects for the Revenue to calculate the tax, the above applies, but where the return is issued after 31st July, then you are allowed two months from the date of issue. If a return is issued after 31st October following the year of assessment and you wish to make a self-assessment claim, there is a three-month period allowable from the date of the return.

Example:

Dr Profitt receives a return for the period 2001/02, which is issued on 4/12/2002. Dr Profitt will be required to file the return on the 4/3/2003 if he wishes to opt for self-assessment and by 4/2/2003 if he elects for the assessment to be made by the Inspector.

Example:

Dr Profitt receives a return for the period 2001/02, which is issued on 4/9/2002. Dr Profitt will be required to file the return on the 31/1/2003 if he wishes to opt for self-assessment and by 4/11/2002 if he elects for the assessment to be made by the Inspector.

If there is a genuine reason why a return cannot be filed on time, it is important to let the Tax Inspector know immediately. It cannot be assumed that your accountant will be able to successfully appeal on your behalf unless it can be demonstrated that there were genuine mitigating circumstances (such as critical illness). It is expected that the Inland Revenue will issue a formal standard of practice concerning returns prior to the commencement of self-assessment for a particular individual but it has been indicated that there will be a 14 day period of grace after the filing date before a penalty is imposed. This should not be treated as an extension for the filing date. A receipt will not be issued, but a statement of account will be which is, in effect, confirmation that the return has been received. If circumstances require, returns could be sent by recorded delivery (ie: if the return is being sent on a date that is close to the expiry filing date). Although the final date for payment is the same as that for completing the return, the payment does not have to accompany the return where this is made earlier than the latest filing date of 31st January.

Many General Practitioners have enjoyed the reasonable freedom and cash advantages available from the old system of the preceding year basis. However, serious consideration must be given to ensuring that tax affairs are brought up to date. Traditionally there may have been various matters that allowed the Practice or its accountants to delay the submission of accounts and therefore defer taxation due to a number of widely interpreted reasons. The current system looks towards bringing the affairs of those that are in tax arrears up-to-date and this could include local offices writing directly to the taxpayer concerned. It should be noted that the Inspector who assists the taxpayer will not be looking at the accuracy of the information contained within the return, but that the return has been completed properly. The fact that the Inspector has assisted in the completion of the return does not mean that the details contained within it will not be subject to a Revenue investigation.

In the past, it was possible for your accountant to deal with your tax affairs by stating 'accounts to follow' or 'as being notified separately'. However, over recent years such returns have been receiving greater scrutiny and under self-assessment such returns are not permissible. The Revenue has recently conceded that returns may be filed as 'complete' when there are genuine reasons for estimated information being used. These returns will still need to be 'fixed' when the actual information becomes available. It should not be used as an excuse for not getting your tax affairs in order. The return must detail amounts specifically in respect of income and gains. The return will not be deemed as made until the missing information is submitted. Therefore, it will not be possible to delay matters and late filing penalties will be issued. Again there may be circumstances where it is not possible to enter accurate figures and estimates must be included. These will be treated as final figures where the figure is accurate to the taxpayer's knowledge and belief, where all reasonable steps have been taken to obtain an actual figure and it is notified appropriately in the return. Such figures will be treated as provisional where it is expected that accurate figures will be provided at a later date. When final figures do become available, they must be notified to the Inspector without delay.

Part of the return process for the Practice will be to extract figures from the Practice Accounts, from the Profit and Loss Account and the Balance Sheet. This summarised information will allow the Practice to be reviewed for any unsatisfactory features that, in turn, will be the basis for selecting the Practice for investigation. Therefore, if any figures in the Practice Accounts are significantly different from the previous year, these should be understood and be explainable before the information is submitted. If this is not done, it could lead to larger accountancy fees to undertake the review work necessary to explain such variances.

In principle it means that the Practice will not actually have to submit full accounts and tax computations with their return, but it is logical that accounts will still need to be prepared in order that the appropriate information can be obtained. In any case, many practices use their accounts when negotiating finance for premises improvements or purchases. As a taxpayer, the General Practitioner is required to sign the return certifying that all the entries detailed are made to the best of his or her knowledge and belief. If the return is not signed, it is not valid. In many cases, the Revenue will not review individual returns, but they may review them retrospectively and, subject to time limits, may impose appropriate penalties and interest charges.

Self-Assessment or Assessment by the Tax Inspector

All returns must contain a self-assessment form unless the option has been taken by the appropriate date to ask for the Inspector to make the assessment. When the option is taken to submit the return by the earlier date, the self-assessment may be omitted and the Inspector will make an assessment on behalf of the taxpayer. If a return is submitted after the appropriate filing date and does not include a self-assessment, the Inspector may make an assessment, but is not obliged to do so. In practice, it is normal for the Inspector to make the assessment, but he does not have to notify the tax in time for payment on the due date unless the return is made by the earlier filing date. If a return is made after 30th September and a tax calculation is not made, although the Revenue will calculate the tax due, they may not notify the taxpayer in time to avoid a penalty. This could result in interest charges on late payments, even though you have not been officially notified of the tax due.

In the case where a return has not been submitted on time, it allows the Inspector to determine the amount of tax due. This determination will be based on the Inspector's understanding of available information and his best belief. It is not possible to appeal against such a determination and any tax determined cannot be postponed. Therefore placing an appeal will not work and the only way to supersede the determination is to file the appropriate return. Until it is superseded the determination is treated for the purposes of recovery for interest, surcharges, etc and for all intents and purposes will be treated as the self-assessment.

Example:

The Tax Inspector makes a determination and establishes the interim payments to be made in the following year. The appropriate time limits are:

Inspectors Determination:
five years from filing date

Self assessment to supersede determination
the later of: a) five years from filing date
                b) 12 months from date of determination

From time-to-time there may be a need to change a return submitted to the Inspector due to an obvious error in arithmetic or error of principle. The Inland Revenue refers to these amendments as 'repairs' and allows for a procedure to make corrections where there is clearly no dispute about the adjustments being made. If you are not happy with the figure supplied by the Inspector, you are entitled to supply your own figure within nine months from actual date that the return is submitted. If this is significantly different to that proposed by the Inspector, there could be grounds for the Inspector to open an investigation.

You are entitled to amend your own self-assessment within 12 months of the actual statutory filing date, which of course will be subject to the actual date of issue of the return. Therefore, where late filing has taken place, this will reduce the amount of time available to submit any amendments. There are no restrictions on the information that can be amended. However, if you are informed that an investigation is already underway, neither the Inspector nor the taxpayer can make subsequent adjustments. Nonetheless, you may inform the Inspector of such adjustments during the investigation notwithstanding that such information is ineffective until the conclusion of the investigation. If you notice an error and do not inform the Inspector without unreasonable delay, you could be deemed as being negligent and suffer the imposition of penalties.

Example:

Dr Profitt submits his tax return for the period 2001/02 on 4/12/2002. It contains an error in the arithmetic. The dates by which it can be officially amended by are as follows;

By the Inspector of Taxes   4/9/2003

By Dr Profitt   31/1/2004

You have a continuing duty to notify the Inspector as soon as the error is discovered. The Inspector has his own timetable for issuing a notification that will trigger an investigation into the accuracy of the amendment. Even when the self-assessment is deemed final, the Inspector can amend it by raising a discovery assessment, but this course of action will only be taken where errors have been made knowingly, fraudulently or negligently on the part of the taxpayer.

If one of the partners or the sole practitioner believes that an error has occurred in the assessment and, as a result, too much tax has been paid, a claim can be made. However the time limit applicable to tax returns is different to that for partnership statements. The time limit for returns is five years from 31st January following the year in question and for partnership statements is five years from the statutory filing date (subject to the date of issue).

Example:

Dr Profitt makes an error in his mathematics that results with him overstating his income by £500 in his 1998/99 return. On the basis that he has overpaid tax, he can make a claim to have the situation corrected by 31st January 2005

As stated previously, the Inspector may wish to raise an assessment under the 'discovery' provisions which allows for adjustments to be made in respect of profits missing assessment, or in circumstances where an assessment is insufficient or excessive relief has been given. To this end the matters concerning your tax affairs are not officially deemed complete until the appropriate time limit has expired. This is just one of the reasons why it is so important to retain all appropriate records, both practice and personal, for the required period.

Postponing Tax and The Appeal Process

In general the process of making an appeal remains as before, although the procedures concerning commissioners' hearings have been formalised since 1994. A commissioner's hearing is a separate review that takes into account both sides of the appeal and determines an outcome accordingly. It is important to note that in certain cases the rights of the commissioners in determining individual cases are limited. A commissioner's hearing, for example, could rule that there were reasonable grounds for a late filing of a return, but they are not empowered to vary the amount involved, but only to set aside the amount involved. In the case where the assessment is reduced following appeal, the tax will be repaid with a proportion of any interest, surcharge or tax geared penalties as if the tax had never been due. However, when the converse happens and there is an increase as a result of an appeal, interest will be charged from the date the tax would have been due. No surcharge will be made providing the full amount is paid within 28 days of the due date.

Example:

Dr Profitt may make an appeal within 30 days, against any of the following:

- The Inspector amends the self assessment during enquiries, because loss of tax is feared

- The Inspector amends the self assessment after enquiries have been completed

- The Inspector amends a partnership statement after enquiries are finished **(Important note:** no appeal is available if the taxpayer amends a self-assessment, or the representative partner amends a partnership statement within 30 days of the notification that the Inspector has completed enquiries. Therefore it is important that you are not pressurised into making amendments to self-assessments with which you do not agree.)

- Discovery assessments are raised

- Discovery assessments to partnership statements are raised

- Inspectors decision on claims outside the return

- Inspectors decision on an error or mistake claim (this appeal will be to the special commissioners)

- Penalties

- Surcharges

Dr Profitt may not make an appeal in the following circumstances:

- Inspector determination in the absence of a return

- Taxpayers own self assessment

- Self-assessment by the Inspector on behalf of the taxpayer

- 'Repairs' made by the Inspector

- An individual partner cannot appeal against amendments made to the self assessment as a result of an amendment made to partnership statement

- Amendment by the taxpayer or the representative partner following the completion of enquiries

When appeals are made, it is possible to apply for the postponement of tax on the basis of the Inspector's assessments during and after enquiries and in the case of discovery assessments. Postponement is not allowed where no appeal process is available and also when an error or mistake claim is made. Therefore, not spending the time to get it right first time could prove to be costly and incur unnecessary costs in respect of payments due as well as costs (such as accountancy fees) to sort out the actual tax position of the Practice.

Interest Payments and The Imposition of Penalties and Surcharges

There are a number of reasons why penalties, interest or surcharges may be incurred by the Practice and in theory all are easily avoidable. The key reasons (and their consequences) are as follows:

Return made late – fixed and daily penalties and tax-geared penalties (those that are set proportionally according to the amount of tax owed) for late personal returns

Notification failure – tax-geared penalty for notifications not received within six months

Incorrect returns, claims etc – tax-geared penalty if return is made fraudulently or negligently

Record keeping – failure to keep records or produce records during an investigation by the Revenue

Interim tax payments – tax-geared penalty for making reduced payments or attempting to avoid making interim payments

Miscellaneous – generally beware! Ensure that the Practice provides all appropriate information and fulfills all obligations

Interest – interest is also charged on penalties if not paid when due

Class 4 National Insurance Contributions – tax-geared penalties are applicable to related class 4 NIC

Let us have a closer look at the potential costs of the avoidable pitfalls illustrated above. Claiming ignorance will not reduce the liability being faced by the Practitioner. A well-publicised campaign by the Inland Revenue has ensured that all taxpayers have been given access to information about the implications of the new system and therefore measures must be adopted immediately if you are to ensure that you do not fall foul of the penalty trap.

For a short delay in filing the return the penalty is £100.00. For a delay of six months or more the penalty is increased by a further £100.00. However the amount of the two penalties cannot exceed the amount of the tax payable on the return. Where there is a delay of 12 months or more it can be up to 100% of the tax due. The latter is in addition to the fixed penalties and additional daily charges may be applicable up to £60.00 per day. The above penalties are limited by the unpaid tax due at the time of the payment date and they can be avoided by making payments on account. Reasonable excuses can be given but are only likely to be accepted where there is a genuine reason such as a delay caused by a postal strike or the serious illness of the responsible partner. Each case will be reviewed on its own merits, however the Revenue is likely to take a more stringent view than it used to about what it considers to be a reasonable excuse.

Be warned! Where the responsible partner fails to make the partnership return on time, the penalties incurred are imposed on all partners. Unlike individual returns, the costs of failing to make appropriate partnership returns is potentially damaging. A short delay will cost £100.00 per partner, a delay of six months or more will cost a further £100.00 per partner and daily penalties will be charged up to £60.00 per day per partner. Reasonable excuses can be used by the representative partner against the fixed charges, but it must be this partner who has the reasonable excuse and not one of the other partners. It is also possible for an individual partner to have a penalty on the partnership return and not on his personal return if the personal return was made on time with an estimate of the partnership income or no tax arises beyond the payments made on account. Therefore, it must be made clear that any partner is at risk of penalties despite having made a personal return on time and having dealt with their own tax obligations. This could be very relevant to recently retired partners or those planning to retire, who will remain at risk during the return periods concerned. In the case of general practice and the nature of incoming partners and retirement of seniors, it may be prudent to review the partnership deed and incorporate indemnities in respect of the continuing partners accordingly.

Example:

Dr Profitt retires from General Practice on 31st March 2001. This happens to be the partnership accounting date and therefore appeared to be a suitable date to retire. Dr Profitt now decides to go on a trip to the Far East. Whilst there he gets involved in a community medical project and knowing that his return will be delayed makes arrangements for his personal return to be filed on time. When he returns home on 3/6/2003, he finds that the partnership return for 2000/2001 has still not been made and a commissioner's hearing had determined on 1/10/2002 that a daily penalty of £20.00 per day would be liable. Therefore, upon his return Dr Profitt would find his penalty to date would be:

Return becomes overdue on 1/2/2002	£100.00
Return now six months overdue on 1/8/2002	£100.00
Daily penalty @ £20.00 (245 days @ £20.00)	£4,900.00
Total penalty to date	£5,100.00

The above example is only illustrative and is not typical of what might happen when a partner retires, but it serves to demonstrate that due care and consideration must be taken when considering a retirement date and almost certainly confirms the view that the partnership deed should be reviewed to ensure that the continuing partners indemnify the outgoing partner against such potential liabilities.

If the representative partner submits an incorrect partnership return, makes a false or incorrect statement, or submits incorrect or false partnership accounts, then a penalty is imposed on all the partners for the period concerned. A penalty only arises when it is due to fraud or neglect of the representative partner or of a person who was a partner during the period concerned. The penalty for each partner will be up to 100% of the difference between a) the tax payable on the partner's own return and b) the tax payable if the return had been correct. An individual partner cannot claim that he or she was unaware of the representative partner's actions and remains liable for the penalty. Remember, an appeal can only be made by the representative partner on behalf of the other partners.

Example:

Dr Profitt has recently completed his qualifying period is enjoying his first few months of parity with the Practice. He is not involved in the accounts preparation side of the Practice and is not aware that the return for year to 31/3/1998 negligently omits one vital source of income. Dr Profitt's tax on the share is calculated at £1,000.00. He is not only liable for a penalty up to £1,000.00 for the error in the return, but also must face interest payments on the late payment of tax. He has no grounds to appeal at all.

Again, the above is an extreme illustration, but serves to identify the potential problems that can occur in a busy practice environment, particularly when there are numerous sources of income and a potentially high tendency to partnership changes. You should be advised that although the penalty system is designed to expedite matters as far as the Revenue is concerned, an understanding of which penalty applies when, means genuine cases of appeal can be supported and unnecessary cost avoided. If you complete a return and include wording such as 'accounts to follow' or 'figures to be advised', you will be deemed as having not completed your return. It will only be considered as being a complete return when the missing information is supplied. Therefore, if this falls outside the filing date for the return, a penalty will be imposed. A return that omits a particular source of income will be treated as being incorrect and is therefore immediately subject to a penalty which can be reduced subject to disclosure, co-operation and the nature of the omission.

Tip: If Dr Profitt knows of a particular source of income, but is unable to quantify it in time for the filing date, he should not omit it from his return, but should contact his local Inspector and enquire whether an extension to the filing date can be arranged or he should provide an estimate and correct the return when a better estimate becomes available or the actual figure is known. This will avoid the potential of receiving an unnecessary penalty

By looking at the way a particular transaction is dealt with in the return, can prevent a situation from be worsened inadvertently. The following example deals with the same issue, but is shown as being dealt with in different ways. The implications are self-evident.

Example:

Dr Profitt realises a capital gain on the sale of a property. The property is sold at a gain during 1997/98. However, by the 31st January 1999, full details about the exact gain are not available and the return is due.

Dr Profitt decides to put the wording 'to be advised' on the return. This return will be incomplete and subject to a late filing penalty.

or:

Dr Profitt submits the return by the filing date, but omits putting any information about the gain. This return is now incorrect and whilst it will not receive a late filing penalty, it will attract a liability for a penalty up to 100% of the tax chargeable on the gain.

or:

Dr Profitt provides an estimate based on known information at the time of filing the return and confirms that the return will be corrected when information becomes available. This return is correct and will not attract a penalty.

Obviously the latter choice in the example is the preferred option, but even that submission must satisfy the criteria that the estimate is correct to the best knowledge and belief of the Doctor and the Inspector must be notified without unreasonable delay when the information does become available. If the estimate is not deemed reasonable the return will be treated as being incorrect or if the information is not reported without unreasonable delay, it too will become incorrect from the date the period of reasonable delay expires.

A final point about potential charges that could be levied against the practice is related to the keeping of proper records and the failure to produce documents during the course of an investigation. All the partners are required to keep records supporting both income notified in the return and for claims made outside the return. There is a penalty for failing to keep these records until the required date. It should be noted that no penalties will be sought for failures prior to the 6th April 1996. The Revenue has also stated that it will not seek to impose penalties as a matter of course, but will look at each individual case accordingly. It is expected that such penalties will be invoked by the Head Office of the Revenue after repeated failure or where records have been deliberately mislaid or destroyed to hamper an investigation. The penalty is up to £3,000.00, although at the time of writing, further guidance is expected about how the Revenue intend to mitigate such penalties. Lastly, the Revenue has the power to ask for documents during the course of an investigation. If you do not comply then there is an initial penalty of £50.00, with additional penalties of up to £30.00 per day if there is a determination by the Inspector and up to £150.00 per day if there is a determination by the Commissioners. If you are unfortunate enough to suffer a penalty and the penalty is not paid within 30 days from the notification of the determination of the penalty, interest will be charged on the amount outstanding.

The purpose of this Annex has not been to frighten the taxpayer into thinking that the new system of self-assessment is draconian in its nature. However, this Annex clearly shows that there is a greater obligation being placed on the individual taxpayer and also on partnerships to get their tax affairs in order and to report more accurately their status. Careful planning and prompt action will avoid any unnecessary penalties or surcharges. Ignorance cannot be accepted as a reasonable excuse and delay in bringing matters to a satisfactory conclusion could be very costly for the Practice.

ANNEX C
TAX PLANNING

This Annex looks at the new regime and covers certain tax planning aspects and the Inland Revenue's current way of thinking. One of the thoughts that may have occurred to the Practice is the change of accounting date. The Practice is of course free to choose its own accounting date, although there are those who wish that all GPs have the same year-end date. The date chosen will probably affect the timing of tax payments, but the principle is that over the life span of the practice, the profits will be taxed once, ie: the Revenue will use the same accounts in the opening years to tax a GP, but overlap relief is credited to the individual once he ceases to be in practice. Changes to accounting dates (except those made in years two or three of a new practice) will only be recognised by the Revenue if specific criteria are met. Let us look at the following practical examples:

When choosing an accounting date the Practice may wish to consider the requirements of the Practice and the fact that reimbursements fall in a quarterly cycle, with many practices electing to have an accounting date at the end of one of the quarter cycles. Others choose 31st March, because it coincides with the local PCT year-end. The timing of the start of a PMS Contract (some commence in October) could dictate the choice of year-end.

Choosing a Tax Date Early in The Tax Year

Choosing an early tax date will mean that the payment of tax is deferred.
Example 1:

Dr Profitt wants to know whether to adopt a year-end of 31st March or 30th April. For the year ended 2004, the tax payment will be calculated as follows :

Profit Earned	Date Balance of Tax Paid
Year to 31st March 2004	31st January 2005
Year to 30th April 2004	31st January 2006

The above example shows a clear advantage for the Practice where profits are rising, but will have an adverse effect if profits fall. Simply, if profits fell, the doctors would be paying tax on higher profits whilst earning at a lower rate. Also, the level of taxable profits will probably be known earlier, which will assist in determining the amount to be paid as the first interim payment (which is due on the 31st January in the year of assessment).

Example 2:

Dr Profitt has to make an interim payment for the tax year 2005/06 on the 31st January 2006. This payment will be based on half the net tax for 2004/05, but can be reduced to half the 2005/06 net tax, if it can be justified. Assuming a 30th April year-end, it should be possible to know whether the current assessment will justify a lower payment:

Accounting Date	Year included in 2005/06 tax liability	First interim payment
31st March	31st March 2006	in tenth month of basis period
30th April	30 April 2005	9 months after end of basis period

By selecting a 30th April year-end date, more time will be available to complete the accounts before they need to submitted to the Inspector. This can mean that the accounts can be completed when your accountant's schedule is less busy and can therefore mean that fees are not at a premium for rushing work through.

Example 3:

How long to prepare the accounts?

Accounting date chosen	Time for production of accounts
31st March	10 months
30th April	21 months

Choosing a Tax Date Later in The Tax Year

When a new practice is created then there will be less profit overlap on commencement and this also applies if there is new partner joining an existing practice. It will also prevent there being a grouping of tax liabilities in the event that the Practice ceases to be or when a partner retires or leaves the partnership. The above will probably be more applicable to a larger partnership where there is the potential for partnership changes is greater, making a later year-end more attractive.

Choosing an Accounting Year-End Date

Firstly, the Practice should take professional advice and weigh up all the options. General Practice is unique compared to most commercial businesses and therefore very often opportunities are squandered or wrong decisions taken. There are many factors which will influence a practice's year-end date, such as the tax year (5th April), financial year (31st March), quarterly reimbursement dates, contract payments etc. In truth, the date chosen is often historic and bears no relationship with the type of issues discussed in this annex. Normally, all factors are weighed up and a decision is made which reflects a compromise of the known factors at the time.

Ways of minimising profit within legitimate bounds include:

- Potential partners are employed before achieving full partnership status (the overlap provisions will apply to this partner on reaching partner status)

- Financing the business by borrowing within the partnership rather than against the personal borrowings of the partners

- Leasing equipment and vehicles rather than purchasing them (not however applicable in the case where equipment is fully reimbursed – there is no double tax relief)

- Paying additional employer's pension contributions or bonuses to staff

- Bringing forward the payment of expenditure items such as practice maintenance costs or stock items

It should be borne in mind that in any case, any year-end date other than 31st March or 5th April will mean that the tax affairs of the partnership will be likely to be more complex, due to the overlap between years.

There has been a lot of publicity about the possibility of making the most advantage of a change of accounting date, but as we will see, the situation is actually quite complicated. It is not simply a matter of deciding to change an accounting date and then submitting accounts accordingly. Unless certain strict criteria are met or the Practice is currently new and in its second or third year, the change will not be recognised for tax purposes. The Practice will continue to be assessed as if no accounting date change had taken place. The year of change is the first year in which the accounts are made up to the new date or if there is a year in which no accounting date falls, it will be that year. Therefore, if the accounts straddle a complete tax year, the accounting rules apply to the tax year straddled and not the year for which the accounts were made up.

The Basic Rules

The basis period for the year of change depends on whether the relevant period is defined as being greater than or less than 12 months. The relevant period is defined as the time to the new accounting date from the end of the previous basis period. Naturally, this will not always be the length of the accounts and the new date may not necessarily be a date to which accounts are actually drawn up (as in the case where the period straddles a complete tax year).

Understanding what constitutes a relevant period is very important. The reason for this is that a short period of account can give rise to a long relevant period. This situation occurs when two sets of accounts end in the same year and are assessed in that year. Conversely, a long period of account can give rise to a short relevant period. This is where the accounts straddle a complete tax year and the new date in that year is within 12 months of the previous accounting date. Where the relevant period is less than 12 months, the basis period is the 12 months to the new date. This will give rise to a profit overlap.

Example 1:

Doctor Profitt changes his accounting date as follows;

Accounts Date	Year	Basis Period
Year to 31/12/1999	1999/00	1/1/99 to 31/12/99
9 months to 30/09/2000	2000/01	1/10/99 to 30/9/00
Year to 30/09/2001	2001/02	1/10/00 to 30/09/01

The above gives rise to a profit overlap of three months (1/10/99 to 31/12/99), which can be relieved later. If the relevant period is longer than 12 months, the basis period is the whole of the relevant period.

Example 2:

Dr Profitt changes his accounting date as follows;

Accounts Date	Year	Basis Period
Year to 31/12/1999	1999/00	1/1/99 to 31/12/99
15 months to 31/03/2001	2000/01	1/1/00 to 31/3/01
Year to 31/03/2002	2001/02	1/4/01 to 31/3/02

If the accounting date conditions are fulfilled, there will be a 15-month basis period for 2001/01. Relief for this assessment may be available for previous profit overlaps.

What Happens with a New Practice?

When the Practice is in its second or third year, the normal rules are applicable except that the following may also apply:

- The accounting date change will be recognised even if the conditions are not fulfilled

- If the new date in year two is within 12 months of commencement, the basis period is the 12 months from commencement

If the new date in year two is 12 months or more from commencement, the basis period is the 12 months to the new date

The Application of the Rules

The following key criteria must be met:

- The first account ending on the new date must not exceed 18 months in length

- The taxpayers must give notice to the Inspector by the 31st January following the year of assessment. In the previous examples, notice must be given by 31st January

2002 of the change that occurred in 2000/01, if there is to be an effective change for tax purposes.

- Either there has been no previous accounting date change recognised for tax in the preceding five years of assessment or,

- The change is because of *bona fide* practical reasons. (A change for tax purposes only is not recognised as a practical reason.)

A change for tax purposes only could mean that the Inspector's decision may not be received for a further 60 days from the filing date and then the decision could be negative. Whilst the decision can be appealed against, notifying the change as early as possible is the best advice.

One of the main reasons for making the rules as they are is to make it difficult to manipulate the rules for tax advantage purposes only. It is also to discourage the use of drawing up accounts over the 18-month period. In the event that the conditions are not met for any reason, the accounting date changes are ignored in the year in which it occurs. The basis period remains the 12 months following that for the preceding year of assessment. In the next year, and thereafter each successive year, the conditions are considered again and, if met, the change is granted then. However, it should be noted that if an accounting date is ignored, returning to the original accounting date will then also be subsequently ignored.

In summary, the Practice should consider the following before looking at changing the accounting date for tax purposes:

If a period is over 18 months, the new accounting date will not be recognised immediately for tax purposes. Therefore, changes to a date which is more than six months later in the tax year will be achieved by a short accounting period

If the notification is given late, it will be considered in a later tax year. This may not be appropriate, as it may not fit with the original tax planning implications of the Practice. A new notification will be required submitted in time

The reason for the need to notify is to allow practices to have a temporary change of accounting date (eg. when partners retire, new partners join etc.) without the need to actually have the date recognised for tax

Practices may not notify the changes at all. This is unlikely to prove advantageous to General Practice.

Changes can be made every six years or at a shorter interval if there are genuine *bona fide* reasons.

The need to consider the appropriate year-end accounting date for the practice is important. However, the special rules and conditions that have been illustrated in this annex are designed to stop advantage being taken by the Practice when profits are seen to rising or falling. Nonetheless, it is an important consideration and a genuine one, whenever there is the possibility of a partnership change. Also any doctor considering starting up a new practice or partnership should seek professional advice about how best to tax plan for the first three years of the Practice.

ANNEX **D**

ANNEX D
GP TAX

This annex provides an overview of the key taxation and allowances that may affect a general practitioner and includes the 2003/2004 rates.

Income Tax and Capital Gains Tax Rates

	2003/04	2002/03	2001/02
Starting Rate on first	£1,960	£1,920	£1,880
Basic Rate on next	£28,540	£27,980	£27,520
Higher rate on taxable income over	£30,500	£29,900	£29,400

Rates differ for:

General Savings and Dividends:

	Other income	Interest	Dividends
Starting	10%	10%	10%
Basic	22%	20%	10%
Higher	40%	40%	32.5%

Allocation of Rate Bands

Taxable income uses up the rate bands in the following order:
- General income
- Savings income
- Dividends

Capital Gains (after annual exemption and taper relief) are added to the total income as the 'top slice' and taxed at the rates applicable to savings income.

Extension of Basic Rate Band

A taxpayer who pays personal or stakeholder pension policy premiums, or cash gifts to charity, increases the basic band by the grossed up equivalent of the payment. This means that more tax is paid at the basic rate and less is paid at the top rate.

Main Personal Allowances

	2003/04	2002/03	2001/02
Personal income tax allowance	£4,615	£4,615	£4,535
Capital Gains Tax annual allowance	£7,900	£7,700	£7,500
Childrens tax credit*	0	£5,290**	£5,200
Blind Persons Allowance	£1,510	£1,480	£1,450

* allowed at 10% only. Reduced by £2 for every £3 by which the parent or partner's income exceeds the higher rate threshold (i.e. NIL if £7,935 is taxed at higher rates in 2002/03)

** £10,490 if a child is born in 2002/03

Age Allowances

	2003/04	2002/03	2001/02
Personal Allowance			
65-74	£6,610	£6,100	£5,990
75 +	£6,720	£6,370	£6,260
minimum *	£4,615	£4,615	£4,535

Married Couples

	2003/04	2002/03	2001/02
Married Couples Allowance **			
65 – 74	£5,565	£5,465	£5,365
75 +	£5,635	£5,535	£5,435
minimum*	£2,150	£2,110	£2,070
Income Limit *	£18,300	£17,900	£17,600

* If the taxpayer's total income exceeds the income limit (extended for gift aid and pension contributions) one half of that excess is deducted from the allowances – first from the personal allowance until the minimum is reached, then from the married couples allowance until the minimum is reached.

** Amount depends on age of older spouse, allowed at 10%, nil if born after 5th April 1935, reduced if marriage took place during the tax year.

Main Personal Reliefs

Rent a room exemption: for letting out part of the taxpayer's only or main residence – gross income of £4,250

Gift aid: on a cash gift to charity, the charity can reclaim 22/78 (28.2%) of the donation from the inland revenue if the donor makes a declaration. The donor increases the basic rate band by the gross gift 100/78. The market value of gifts of land or quoted shares can be deducted from taxable income for full tax relief, and the charity pays no tax on the income.

Employee Taxation

Employment income is charged to both income tax as general income and to Class 1 National Insurance Contributions. Tax and NIC are normally paid by the employer through the PAYE system, but an employee whose tax is not fully paid should complete a tax return and settle the liability as described above.

If the tax underpaid is up to £2,000 and the 2001/2002 was submitted by the 30/9/2002 or by the 30/12/2002 if filed by the internet, the underpayment can be settled through PAYE for 2003/04 rather than being collected on 31st January 2003.

Class 1 NIC rates 2003/04

Employers and employees both contribute. Employee contributions are capped for income above the upper earnings limit (UEL).

	Week	Month	Year
Primary Threshold PT	£89.00	£385.00	£4,615.00
Upper Earnings Limit UEL	£595.00	£2,579.00	£30,940.00
Secondary Threshold	£89.60	£385.00	£4615.00

No NIC are payable by the employee or employer up to the primary threshold.

Earnings between the LEL and the PT must be reported by the employer and the employee receives credit towards the State Pension, but no NIC are payable.

Rates of NIC on earnings above the PT depend on whether the employee is within the State Earnings-Related Pension Scheme (SERPS) or whether the employee has contracted out using a final salary or money purchase scheme.

	SERPs		Salary Related		Money Purchase	
	Contracted in Table A		Contracted out Table D		Contracted out Table F	
	EEs	ERs	EEs	ERs	EEs	ERs
PT - UEL	11%	12.8%	9.4%	9.3%	9.4%	11.8%
Above UEL	1%	12.8%	1%	12.8%	1%	12.8%

Contracting out employers receive a special rebate on earnings between the LEL and the PT. A person with more than one employment can defer the payment of some or all employee NIC until after the end of the tax year, when the total amount payable can be checked and limited to the annual maximum

Benefits in Kind

Benefits in kind are usually valued at a cash equivalent value and are then charged to income tax on the employee and class 1A NIC (at 12.8%) on the employer. The cash equivalent is generally based on the cost to the employer of providing the benefit, but the following are charged according to a statutory methodology.

Cars provided by the employer: a percentage of the original list price of the car, depending on the CO_2 emissions rating of the car:

	2002/03	2003/04	2004/05
15% of list price	to 169g/km	to 159g/km	to 149g/km
1% addition	170, 175 etc	160, 165 etc	150, 155 etc
max 35% benefit	over 264g/km	over 254g/km	over 244g/km

For diesel cars add 3% (minimum is 18%, maximum is still 35%). There is no discount for the level of business mileage or the age of the car, but deduct employee contributions for private use.

Fuel provided by the employer for private use in a company car is charged according to the following table, without reduction for contributions unless all private fuel is paid for by the employee:

Engine CC	Petrol Engine	Diesel Engine
1400cc or less	£2,240	£2,850
1401cc – 2000cc	£2,850	£2,850
over 2000cc	£4,200	£4,200

Vans provided by the employer are charged at a flat rate of £500 (£350 if the van is older than four years at the end of the tax year).

Loans of money of over £5,000 are charged on the excess of the official rate (5%) over any interest actually paid by the employee to the employer.

Use of assets is charged at 20% of the original cost of the assets to the employer or the value when first made available to the employee, less any amount paid by the employee for private use.

Main Exempt Benefits in Kind

There are many benefits in kind that are not charged to tax. The following list is not exhaustive, but may be of interest.

Providing a mobile phone, even with private use (but paying the bills on the employees own phone remains chargeable)

Lending computer equipment where the 20% charge would be up to £500 (ie: a value of up to £2,500 if there is only private use).

The provision of 'green transport' such as works buses or the use of a bicycle for commuting.

Exempt Mileage Allowances: Use of Employee's Own Car

First 10,000 miles	Extra miles	Each passenger
40p	25p	5p

Exempt Fuel Only Allowances: Company Car

Engine CC	Petrol Engine	Diesel Engine
1400cc or less	10p	9p
1401cc – 2000cc	12p	9p
over 2000cc	14p	12p

Other Exempt Payments To or For Employees

i) mileage allowances of up to 24p per mile for business use of the employees motorcycle or 12p per mile for pedal cycle

ii) contributions to approved pension schemes

iii) payments up to £5 a night when staying away for 'personal incidental expenses' (£10 if abroad).

Employee Share Schemes

Generally, employees are charged income tax on the value of shares that they are given or issued by their employer, less any amount paid for the shares. This applies to free shares and to shares acquired under share option schemes. NIC is also charged if the company is quoted so the shares can be easily sold. If the employer operates one of these revenue approved schemes, the tax charged may be eliminated, reduced or deferred.

Share Incentive Plans

i) free shares to £3,000 per year

ii) partnership shares (employee buys with pre-tax salary) maximum £1,500 per year, employer can match with up to two more for each

iii) shares left in the scheme for at least five years will mean no income tax or capital gains tax on the value when they leave the scheme.

Enterprise Management Incentives

Small trading companies can grant options to buy up to £100,000 worth of shares to selected employees. Company share option plans can be granted to employees to buy up to £30,000 of shares. Approved savings-related share options plan are where employees contribute to a save as you earn plan (maximum £250 per month) to save money needed to exercise options. With approved option schemes, the employee pays Capital Gains Tax on the sale of the shares rather that income tax on exercising the options. The Capital Gains charge is likely to be smaller and later than the income tax or NIC liability.

Capital Gains Tax

Disposal of assets chargeable to Capital Gains Tax involve quite complicated calculations. If the asset was owned before April 1998, the cost is adjusted for the effect of inflation up to that month before working out the gain. For assets bought since, the gain is generally the excess of proceeds over cost. Capital Gains Tax is reported, taxed and paid in conjunction with income tax.

Taper Relief

For disposals since April 1998, gains are reduced according to the length of time for which the asset has been owned. Assets owned before 1998, only count for the time since 6 April 1998, plus one year for a non-business asset which was owned on 17th March 1998.

Business assets have a more generous rate of Taper Relief.

Investment Reliefs

The main tax incentives for investments are as follows:

i)   income tax deduction for amounts invested, the rebate is fixed at 20% or at the taxpayers marginal rate

ii) tax exemption on the income from the source

iii) tax exemption on gains arising

iv) repayment of tax credits on dividends arising

v)   the ability to defer capital gains on other disposals until the new investment is sold

The main types of tax-advantaged investments are:

ISA – Individual savings account

TESSA – Tax exempt special savings account

PEP – Personal equity plan

EIS – Enterprise investment scheme

VCT – Venture capital trust

PPPs – Personal pension plans (also stakeholder pensions)

Pension Contributions

Age at the beginning of 2003/04	PPP max %
Up to 35	17.5
36-45	20
46-50	25
51-55	30
56-60	35
61 and over	40

The highest for the year or for the last five years can be used to justify the Personal Pension Plan (PPP) contribution for the current year.

ANNEX E:
KEY FINANCIAL DATES FOR 2003

April

5th   End of Tax Year

5th   Cut off date for income and gains between 02/03 and 03/04

19th   Employers pay PAYE for quarter or month March 2003

19th   IR35 tax due

May

3rd   Employers submit P46(car) form showing quarters changes to company cars

19th   Employers pay PAYE for month April 2003

19th   Employers submit 02/03 year end returns to revenue, P14, P35, P38, P38A

31st   Employers send 02/03 P60 to employees

June

19th   Employers pay PAYE for month May 2003

July

5th   Deadline for Tax Credit to commence from start of 3rd quarter

6th   Employers send P9D and P11D returns to Revenue, P11D to employees

19th   Employers pay PAYE for quarter or month June 2003

19th   Employers pay class 1A NIC for 02/03

31st   2ND PAYMENT OF ACCOUNT RE 02/03 SELF-ASSESSMENT

August

2nd Employers submit P46(car) form showing quarters changes to company cars

19th Employers pay PAYE for month July 2003

September

19th Employers pay PAYE for month August 2003

30th FILE 02/03 RETURN TO TAKE ADVANTAGE OF REVENUE CALCULATION AND CODING OUT OF SCHEDULE E UNDERPAYMENTS

October

1st Corporation tax payday for companies with 31st December 2002 year end

19th Employers pay PAYE for quarter or month September 2003

November

2nd Employers submit P46(car) form showing quarters changes to company cars

19th Employers pay PAYE for month October 2003

December

19th Employers pay PAYE for month November 2003

31st Corporation tax filing deadline for companies with 31st December 2002 year end

January

1st Corporation tax payday for companies with 31st March 2003 year end

19th Employers pay PAYE for quarter or month December 2003

February

2nd   Employers submit P46(car) form showing quarters changes to company cars

19th   Employers pay PAYE for month January 2004

28th   Deadline for payment of balance of 02/03 tax TO AVOID SURCHARGE

March

19th   Employers pay PAYE for month February 2004

31st   Corporation tax filing deadline for companies with 31st March 2003 year end

ANNEX F
THE BUDGET: SPRING 2003

What It Means To You

The budget speech was delayed this year, presumably because of the war with Iraq, but most of the changes this year were already announced in last year's speech and therefore their impact has been slightly lessened. Those points that may affect GPs are detailed below:

Significant Points

- Income tax rates and main allowance are frozen

- NIC rates are increased by 1% for employee and employer

- New working tax credit and child tax credit introduced from 6/4/03

- New Pension credit from October

- Inheritance tax and pension schemes have no significant changes

- Introduction of new Child Trust Fund - £250 for every child at birth, to spend at age 18

- Very small increases in 10% and 22% income tax bands (inflation only).

Tax Tip 1

The new tax credits depend on making a claim, which can only be backdated by three months. To establish entitlement from the start of the new system, a form has to be submitted by 5th July 2003.

Tax Tip 2

The new NIC increases can be hurtful. Look at ways of using either the PMS or new GMS Contract to establish ways of mitigating them. This is particularly relevant with the recruitment and retention of salaried GPs.

Tax TRAP 1

If you currently have the benefit of a company car, are you sure that the benefit of the car and fuel are worth the tax that you pay?

Tax Tip 3

Doctors who own property or act as landlords should see some good news in respect of lower Capital Gains Tax implications.

Tax TRAP 2

At present the rules regarding leases may change following consultation resulting in significantly higher charges. It may be prudent to take on a lease sooner than the changes being implemented.

Tax Tip 4

Another year is available for the purchase of computer equipment with 100% writing down allowance available.

Tax TRAP 3

Plan to purchase computer equipment now, the above measure may not be available from next year.

INDEX

Remortgage: 46

Rent: 46-47, 80, 124, 126-7, 129

Return on Equity: 112-115

Return on Total Assets: 112-115

Rural Practice Allowance: 13

Salaried Option: 50

Schedule D: 65, 76, 88

Schedule E: 65, 182

Self-assessment: 13, 19, 23, 43,
49, 57-58, 119, 121, 146-154,
160, 181

Seniority Payments: 9, 50, 130

Sickness Allowance: 13

Software: 23-24

Staff Pension Scheme: 73

Stakeholder Pensions: 125, 172, 178

State Earnings-Related Pension
Scheme (SERPS): 174

Statement of Fees and
Allowances (SFA): 6-7, 79, 99

Statement of Income and
Expenditure: 101, 102

Statutory Sick Pay (SSP): 68, 71

Statutory Maternity Pay (SMP): 68, 71

Study Leave: 13

Surgery, Minor: 12, 84

Surveillance, Child Health: 11

Target Payments: 39

Tax Codes: 59, 65, 69, 72

Tax Inspector: 92, 102, 147, 149-150

Tax Rebate: 65, 119, 178

Tax Tables: 65, 67, 69, 72-73

Taxpayers' Charter: 89

Teaching Allowance: 12

Total Assets: 105, 110-115

Trainee Practitioner Payments: 13

Training: 10, 11, 49, 52,, 130

Trial Balance: 23, 24

Turnover: 17, 117

Upper Earnings Limit: 64, 173, 174

Use of Home: 89, 91-93

Visits, Nights: 12-13

Vouchers: 20-21, 101, 122, 145

Wholly and Exclusively Rule: 87, 88, 130

Working Capital: 111-115, 129